Riding the Wind

Your Life in the Holy Spirit

Riding
the
Wind

Your Life in the
Holy Spirit

Everett L. Fullam

Creation  **House**
Altamonte Springs, Florida

© Copyright 1986 by Strang Communications Company
Altamonte Springs, Florida 32714
All rights reserved
Printed in the United States of America
Library of Congress Number: 86-63197
ISBN Number: 0-88419-196-6

Unless otherwise noted, the Scripture quotations contained
herein are from the Revised Standard Version of the Bible
copyrighted 1946, 1952, 1971 by the Division of Christian
Education of the National Council of the Churches of Christ
in the USA, and are used by permission. All rights reserved.

To my mother, Mary F. Fullam, now in her 95th year—who was the first to turn my heart to the Lord and set my feet in the direction of the kingdom, this book is lovingly dedicated.

Contents

Foreword

We All
Call Him "Terry"

I suppose most of us know our friends in a variety
of roles, and this is so in my relationship with Everett
L. Fullam.

I knew him first as just a name, one which kept pop-
ping up as I began researching the early days of the
renewal movement. I then heard him speak; what an
experience that was! The Rev. Fullam had a special gift
in encouragement. I eventually came to know him in
my own editorial and publishing life. But...not one of
these represents the first role he played in my life.

It is the same with everyone I know who has had on-
going contact with Everett L. Fullam. And all of us sym-
bolize our special relationship with him in something
of the same manner. Just ask staffers at St. Paul's
Episcopal Church, Darien, Connecticut, where he is rector, how they think of their pastor. Or ask his editors,
publishers, television emcees, radio interviewers and

technicians. Ask anybody who works with Everett L. Fullam what they call him and almost always the answer is "Terry."

Now I see this as important because it points up the primary role of Terry Fullam in people's lives. He has the aura about him of a friend. He is "Terry" my friend first; only later is he a teacher or writer or preacher.

This fact had a lot to do with my attitude as I sat down to read *Riding the Wind*. It was Terry speaking to me, Terry my friend who was never so experienced in the life of the Spirit that he forgot his reader...me, you. We need frequently to be taken by the hand. That's the gesture a friend makes. Terry is a teacher who does this; he leads not by talking to us so much as by walking *with* us.

Let me give an example from his book. Most of us, I suppose, and this is true of me, have a problem reconciling what we should be with what we are. We are experiencing, in other words, a problem with the age-old issue of holiness. On a recent automobile trip I tuned the car radio to a sermon where the preacher was scolding his audience roundly for yielding to temptation. His point was well taken, but it was not very helpful because he didn't then go on to tell me how to deal with the problems of temptation. All he did was exhort me to be stronger, to become perfect, now, today, or I would have no place in the kingdom of God.

Not so with Terry. As a friend, Terry teaches me that the temptations I face are never *caused* by God but they are *allowed* by Him, and always for a purpose. God is in control of temptations, says Terry, as they come into my life. He regulates the degree of the trials and He allows Satan to go only so far. Then He always supplies a way out, through the work of the Holy Spirit. The whole is for a purpose, not to earn salvation but to make me stronger as I walk into the work He has prepared for me to do.

Now that is hand-holding. It is walking with me through what I know to be unpleasant facts about myself, and it is teaching me the way out.

Terry does this throughout his book. He takes me on a search for the person of the Spirit. Then, like any good friend, he challenges me to look honestly at the shortfalls of my walk with the Lord. He uses his own experience and insights from a life of prayer to take me through the obstacle course—to the toughened, more useful person he knows God intended all along.

—*John Sherrill*

Part One

The Gift of God

Chapter One

The Thirst Quencher

A man and a woman sitting by a well, talking about their thirst—such a mundane scene hardly seems appropriate as the setting for one of the two greatest conversations in history. But the man was Jesus, and as He asked for water that would soothe His dry throat, His new acquaintance was looking for water that would satisfy her spirit. The result was a dialogue that is important to us all.[1]

Jesus and His disciples had been traveling north from Jerusalem to Galilee, and the most direct route took them through the territory of Samaria. At noon, when they'd come near the town of Sychar, they had stopped to eat. While the disciples went into town to buy food, Jesus sat down to rest beside a well built by Jacob some 1800 years earlier.

Generations of travelers had stopped here before to refresh themselves and gather strength to continue their journeys, so a stranger wasn't an unusual sight to the woman who had come to draw water. But it *was* unusual that He would speak to her, even to beg a drink; she was a woman and a Samaritan. No wonder she answered His request with another question: "Why are you, a Jew, asking me, a woman and a Samaritan, for water? Don't you know that the Jews have no dealings with the Samaritans?"

Now these "no dealings" were ancient and deep-seated, going back seven centuries to the time when Assyria conquered the Northern Kingdom of Israel, capturing and scattering ten of the twelve tribes beyond the Tigris and Euphrates valleys. To reduce the chance of revolt, the Assyrians had allowed only the "undesirables" of the conquered Jewish nation to remain in Palestine: the sick, the unskilled, the old. Over the centuries these remaining Jews intermarried with pagans the Assyrians had brought in to work the land. They became known as Samaritans, and the Jews who returned from exile to live in the South hated these Northerners as heretics and half-breeds.

In Jewish eyes, the Samaritans' heretical status was confirmed by their refusal to accept as Scripture any writings but the first five books of the Old Testament. Worse yet, the Samaritans appointed their own priests and worshipped on Mount Gerizim in Samaria instead of worshipping at the temple in Jerusalem.

In Jesus' day, devout Jews wouldn't even walk through the territory of Samaria. To get from Jerusalem to Galilee, they would go east on the Jericho Road, cross the Jordan River, walk north, and then cross back over the river into Galilee. So Jesus' mere presence at that well was a sign that He was an unusually unprejudiced man.

Jesus' answer to the woman, however, showed that He was more than just unusual: "If you knew the gift of God, and who it is that is saying to you, 'Give me a drink,' you would have asked him, and he would have given you living water."

Even so, the woman apparently had no idea yet that Jesus was ever so gently changing the topic of conversation away from H_2O and toward her inward thirst. She answered: "Where do you get that living water? Are you greater than our father Jacob, who gave us the well?"

Jesus continued: "Every one who drinks of this water will thirst again. But whoever drinks of the water that I shall give him will never thirst."

Still the woman failed to catch on. What a boon, she probably thought, to have my own artesian well, especially since I have to come here at noon when the rest of the women aren't around. As the town outcast, she was anxious to avoid the scorn of her neighbors.

Instead of explaining what He was talking about, however, Jesus asked the woman to go get her husband. He knew her need. Caught off guard, she probably stammered and stuttered and finally said, "Well, uh, the fact is...I have no husband."

Jesus replied, "You are right in saying, 'I have no husband'; for you have had five husbands, and he whom you now have is not your husband." Now He was getting close—too close.

In John 2:24-25, the Gospel writer notes that Jesus needed no one to tell Him what was in people's hearts because He knew perfectly well what was there. Jesus knew the thirst of this woman's spirit was like that of the psalmists': "As a hart longs for flowing streams, so longs my soul for thee, O God. My soul thirsts for God, for the living God"[2]; "O God, thou art my God, I seek thee, my soul thirsts for thee; my flesh faints for thee, as in a dry and weary land where no water is."[3]

The difference, of course, was that the psalmists knew what would quench their thirst; this Samaritan woman did not. Her insatiable thirst had driven her from one sexual relationship to another—seeking but not finding something that would touch the deepest level of her being.

Eternity in the Minds of Humankind

An obscure little verse in Ecclesiastes 3 says that God has put "eternity" in the minds of humankind. I suspect it means that God fashioned us so that we can never find permanent satisfaction in anything this world has to offer.

Most of the time we operate under a great delusion: We imagine that if we had more money or a more prestigious job or more power, we would be satisfied. I'm not saying, of course, that this world doesn't have its satisfactions; only that they can't touch the deepest core of our hearts. They can't permanently satisfy. As Saint Augustine said to God: "You have made us for Yourself, and our heart is restless until it rests in You." We were created for a relationship with Him, and a thirst for that relationship drives us, even when we don't realize it's there.

Years ago I read a novel by Somerset Maugham called *The Razor's Edge*. The lead character, Larry Darrell, was a young man who, more than most, recognized this thirst. It drove him all over the world—from the United States to Paris to a Tibetan monastery and back again to Paris. But the story ended with Larry still searching for the water that would quench the thirst of his spirit.

Even Solomon, known as the wisest and one of the wealthiest men ever to live, eventually realized that nothing in the created world would fill the void—not the work of his hands, not the bodies of his six hundred wives, not the comfort of his beautiful homes and landscaped parks. Nothing. In Ecclesiastes 2:10-11 he laments:

"Whatever my eyes desired I did not keep from them; I kept my heart from no pleasure, for my heart found pleasure in all my toil, and this was my reward for all my toil. Then I considered all that my hands had done and the toil I had spent in doing it, and behold, all was vanity and a striving after wind, and there was nothing to be gained under the sun."

Solomon wanted to find out what a good life would be, and in that respect, I suspect he was like every one of us.

This thirst can drive people ideologically as well. The major religions of the world are people's own attempts to satisfy their longings for God. Buddhism, Hinduism, Islam—all contain some truth, but they don't provide the fullness of a relationship with God.

I've never heard any evidence to convince me that this thirst for living water isn't universal. Sometimes, as with the Samaritan woman, it takes a while to rise to our consciousness; but even people who appear to be contented or successful instinctively know that something is missing. The voice of emptiness within can't be silenced.

My parish is located in Darien, Connecticut, a "bedroom community" of New York City. We have many corporate executives in our parish, and a number of new members come to us as others are transferred out of the area. So twice a year we have a dinner to welcome our new members, during which we invite them to say a bit about themselves and how their life within our fellowship is progressing.

Again and again on this occasion, up-and-coming corporate executives tell of their "God-shaped vacuum" and how it was filled as they received Jesus in the power of the Spirit. The common thread through each individual tale is of hiding for years behind a mask of self-sufficiency and control, "having it all together," until they encounter an atmosphere of acceptance, where they are free to be who they really are. They find that they can gradually let down masks and be vulnerable, that nobody expects them to be perfect, and that nobody around them is perfect either!

This happens all the time—and it's a transforming experience. The new members even look different after awhile: Their faces show less strain, they smile more readily, and they become less guarded in their approach to others. As their lives become permeated with the love of Christ, it overflows into every area, bringing new discoveries, new directions and new relationships.

The Water of Life

What precisely is the water of life Jesus promised both to that woman and to anyone who is thirsty in spirit?

If you remember, Jesus changed the topic of conversation from physical water to spiritual water with the words: "If you knew the gift of God...." We learn the identity of that gift in the Acts of the Apostles, the book that tells the history of the early church. There, the Holy Spirit or the Spirit of Jesus is four times referred to as "the gift of God." Consequently, the consecration prayer in our modern *Book of Common Prayer* calls the Holy Spirit our Lord's first gift to us. If you know the Holy Spirit, then—if you know Jesus—He gives you the water that not only refreshes but saves from death. Later in John's Gospel, we read that "in the last day, that great day of the feast, Jesus stood and cried, saying, 'If any man thirst, let him come unto me, and drink.'"[4] Biblical scholars agree that John is referring here to the Feast of the Tabernacles.

On the last day of that festival, two great earthenware jars filled with water were placed at the temple door, one on either side. As Psalms 42 and 63 were read (these are the two quoted above that speak of thirst for God), those jars were slowly emptied so that the crowds who had come to celebrate saw the water pouring out across the pavement. I can just imagine Jesus raising His voice above the wet stones and saying, "If anyone thirsts, let him come to Me and drink."

That is an extraordinary statement. The prophets of Israel never talked that way about themselves. They said, "Turn unto the Lord and He will heal you." The apostle Paul never claimed to be the source of refreshment. He said, "I preach Jesus."

But it was Jesus who said, "I am the living bread which came down from heaven; if any one eats of this bread, he will live for ever."[5] He forthrightly claimed to be able to satisfy the deepest hunger and thirst of our spirits. He alone is the One who can provide meaning and purpose and significance in our lives.

Just as Jesus told the Samaritan woman that the water He gave would "well up to eternal life," He proclaimed from the steps of the temple at the Feast of Tabernacles that whoever believes in Him would have streams of living water flowing out of their hearts. In fact, John goes out of his way to explain what Jesus was talking about: "Now this he said about the Spirit, which those who believed in him were to receive."[6]

I'm reminded of an occasion several years ago when I was asked by the Anglican bishop of Iran to go to that beautiful country and conduct a series of missions. One day as I was flying across the desert, I glanced down and saw ahead of us what looked like a large black square. In the midst of such desolate terrain, I knew this wasn't a natural phenomenon; yet there were no houses or tents around it or even any roads leading to it. When I pointed the area out and asked the flight attendant what it was, she explained that it had been an experiment of the government.

"A while back," she said, "they were drilling for oil. They didn't find it, but they did strike an artesian well. So they capped it and laid pipes across the sand for one square mile. The pipes had tiny holes in them, and when they turned on the water, it flowed out as a misty spray. Within one month, green shoots had started to push through the sand."

Before I could ask who had planted the seeds that grew, she hastened to tell me that no one had planted anything; the winds had blown in seeds which had long before mixed with the sand. They'd lain dormant—until the water made the life within them come bursting forth.

"That was about three years ago," she added. "What you see now is a jungle that is one square mile."

All because the soil drank of the water—just water.

Come, Drink

The organized church is not the answer to human restlessness or hunger or thirst. In fact, down through

22

history and even today, the church has had a way of placing itself between Jesus and the people He wants to refresh and satisfy. The institution has often said or strongly implied, "If you're baptized, you're in"; "If you put enough offering in the plate, you're fine"; "If you come every Sunday, you'll be blessed."

But it's not enough to be in the presence of refreshment; we have to take it within ourselves. We could stand beside a banquet table laden with nutritious food and still starve to death. We could lie beside a stream of fresh, pure water, yet die of thirst.

If we have a glass of water in our hand but don't put it to our lips and swallow, our thirst will not be quenched. The living water—the Spirit of Jesus Himself—is what the church needs, and what individuals in the church need, to be brought back to life.

The last chapter of the last book of the Bible refers again to our thirst and to God's gift of water. Revelation 22:17 says: "The Spirit and the Bride [the church] say, 'Come.' And let him who hears say, 'Come.' And let him who is thirsty come, let him who desires take the water of life without price."

What a way to end the Scriptures! The Spirit issues an invitation to our spirit—"Come...Come...Come"—just as Jesus, on the steps of the temple, said, "If anyone thirsts, let him come to me and drink" of the water that's not for sale, but free.

In the remaining pages of this book, I want to talk more about the Holy Spirit and how He works in and upon the lives of men and women, boys and girls. This may seem to many an unusual topic. I remember the archbishop of Canterbury telling me, for example, that his personal library had always been full of books about

God the Father, Creator of heaven and earth, and about God the Son, our Savior and Lord; but only recently had he built up a section about the Third Person of the Trinity, the Holy Spirit, the Lord and giver of life.

I suspect his library simply reflects how Christian writers and thinkers throughout church history have tended to neglect the Spirit. But we are living in a new day, when the ministry of the Holy Spirit is being recognized and talked about. Admittedly, the Holy Spirit's desire is not to attract attention to Himself; He always wants to focus our attention on the Lord Jesus (Jesus said of the Spirit, "He will glorify me"[7] and "He will bear witness to me"[8]). Nevertheless, we must understand how the Spirit has worked and is working to direct people's hearts—and spirits—toward God.

Chapter Two

The Giver of Life

If one of history's two greatest conversations was the dialogue at Jacob's well, the other is an exchange recorded immediately before it in the third chapter of John's Gospel. Here Jesus explains our entrance into the kingdom of God to a strictly orthodox and influential Jew named Nicodemus. This well-known story, in which Jesus says, "You must be born again," is frequently misinterpreted so that the marvelous and encouraging point of it is completely missed.

Questions, Answers

It was late in the evening—after most of the city of Jerusalem had gone to bed—and Nicodemus, a member of the Jewish ruling council, left his home in search of Jesus, the teacher and miracle worker. Nicodemus wanted to see and hear for himself, but privately and perhaps confidentially. Maybe he wasn't ready to declare himself a follower; his search was sincere, but he needed more time.

Although I've never sought advice under the cover of darkness, I can relate to such concerns. Some time ago, the presiding bishop asked me to meet twelve prominent Episcopal clergy—chastened liberals, including the deans of five cathedrals and many former leaders in the civil rights movement. He said it was kind of a Nicodemus meeting: They wanted to meet on neutral territory and they didn't want anyone to know that they were inquiring about life in the Holy Spirit. We had a wonderful meeting, as did Nicodemus and Jesus.

So I have some idea of what Nicodemus may have been feeling when he began by acknowledging what he had seen and heard: "Rabbi, we know that you are a teacher come from God; for no one can do these signs that you do, unless God is with him." Some people think that Nicodemus was trying to ingratiate himself with Jesus, but I don't believe that for a moment. In chapter 2, right before the beginning of this story, John says that many people had seen Jesus' miraculous signs, or miracles, and I'm sure Nicodemus was one of those curious onlookers who had concluded that no one could do this work unless God was with him.

Even so, I'm more fascinated with Jesus' reply than with Nicodemus's greeting. Jesus didn't say, "Why, thank you very much." Knowing what was in the heart of any man or woman, Jesus immediately addressed the need He saw in Nicodemus, even before any questions were asked or needs expressed. Jesus said, "Truly, truly, I say to you, unless one is born anew, he cannot see the kingdom of God.'' Although Nicodemus hadn't mentioned the kingdom of God, Jesus abruptly moved the conversation in that direction, toward the perceived need.

Nicodemus, not having any idea what Jesus was talking about, asked: "How can a man be born when he is old? Can he enter a second time into his mother's womb and be born?''

Here and in several other conversations, including the one with the Samaritan woman beside Jacob's well, Jesus used an unusual teaching technique. Most teachers who sense that their students aren't getting the point will stop, back up, rephrase and come at the subject again from a second and maybe a third angle. That's what I would have done. At this point I would have said, "No, Nicodemus, that's not what I meant. I wasn't talking about reentering your mother's womb in a literal fashion."

But Jesus kept right on going, allowing Nicodemus to struggle with a tendency to over-literalize because He wanted him to wrestle with the force of the radical, startling, vigorous image of spiritual rebirth. Jesus said, "Truly, truly, I say to you, unless one is born of water and the Spirit, he cannot enter the kingdom of God.''

In this expansion of the topic at hand, Jesus changed verbs: from *seeing* the kingdom of God to *entering* the kingdom. In English, the word *see* has two meanings. If I say that I see a tree outside my window, you would understand that I'm speaking of visual sight. With my eyes I see the tree. But I might also use the word in a sentence such as "I see what you mean.'' In that sense *see* is interchangeable with the word *understand*, and I think that's the way Jesus was using it here: Unless you are born again, you cannot understand or enter the kingdom of God.

The Kingdom of God

What is the kingdom of God? It was clearly the focus of Jesus' entire ministry. The Gospel of Mark records the first words of Jesus' ministry to be "The kingdom of God is at hand; repent."[1] Over and over again, His parables began, "The kingdom of God is like unto...." In the Sermon on the Mount, He said, "Seek first his kingdom and his righteousness, and all these things shall be yours as well."[2]

God's kingdom is the sphere of His sovereignty. It's the reign or rule of God, and it takes place in the hearts of men and women and children. It's not a place: He said His kingdom was not of this world.[3] It's not bound by time: Abraham, Isaac and Jacob were in the kingdom; when Jesus was on earth He said that the kingdom was then among them; and He prayed that the kingdom might come—in the future. The kingdom of God is in fact the key concept of the entire Bible, tying together everything from Genesis to Revelation.

So what is God doing on earth for heaven's sake? He's establishing a kingdom within people's hearts that ultimately will replace the kingdoms of this world.

Jesus went on to explain further to Nicodemus what this spiritual rebirth and entering the kingdom of God was all about: "That which is born of the flesh is flesh, and that which is born of the Spirit is spirit." The natural life we receive from our parents will not understand or be part of the kingdom of God; the Holy Spirit alone can cause us to be birthed into this spiritual kingdom.

What does it mean to enter the kingdom? Those who don't enter are doomed to live their lives without ever finding ultimate meaning, without finding a sense of genuine fulfillment, without quenching their thirst. The eternal significance of it in the here and now is terribly important.

Jesus said: "Not every one who says to me, 'Lord, Lord,' shall enter the kingdom of heaven, but he who does the will of my Father who is in heaven."[4] One of the devastating lies that the evil one has successfully planted in our hearts is that God's will for us is surely dreadful. Most people fear the will of God. They think God delights in snatching away their happiness and making life dreary.

But just the opposite is true. God's will for our lives is exactly what we most desire: a life of significance, a life of meaning, a life of success; and these qualities can be found only when we submit to His will rather than to our own, when we enter the kingdom of God by allowing Him to rule in our hearts. That's the place where everything begins to come together.

Before people enter the kingdom, they fear the rule of God; they fear surrendering to the Holy Spirit. They don't understand that in the will of God are light, strength and joy. They think that losing their wills and surrendering to the will of Christ will be the end of them. But Jesus said that just the reverse is true: Those who try to save their lives will lose it; those who lose their lives for Christ's sake paradoxically find it.[5]

Lee Buck is a good example of this truth. He's a member of our parish who today is a partner in ministry and a full-time evangelist. Lee's story is about a climb to the top of the corporate ladder, one hard-won rung at a time, with a combination of brains and brashness. He has one of the strongest wills around—just ask him!—so surrender to Jesus was the last thing on Lee's mind; he was a scoffer at the simplicity of the message.

But the love of Christ eventually broke through the barriers of fear and mistrust. That love was poured out to him through the members of a weekly Bible study and the consistent witness of the Word of God, until one week, this senior vice president of the New York Life Insurance Company tearfully told Jesus, "I'm not much, but whatever I am, You can have me."

God knew what He wanted from Lee and how He would use Lee full-time to bring many into His kingdom. He's changed Lee's business from selling life insurance to "offering eternal life assurance" to people all over the world. Lee lost his corporate life for Christ's sake, taking early retirement so that he could find a fuller life in the service of Jesus, bringing people into the kingdom.

Entering the Kingdom

How do you enter the kingdom? Jesus said it is through being "born of water and the Spirit."[6] Some people have interpreted this passage to mean that the water refers to natural birth, fluids being instrumental in that physical process. They say this and then point out the parallels in the following verse, which refers to flesh giving birth to flesh. Other groups interpret being born of water to refer to water baptism.

Although there is some evidence for both these interpretations, I have yet a third understanding: that the water refers to cleansing and purification. I base this interpretation on Ephesians 5:25-26, where Paul speaks of the relationship between husbands and wives and Christ's relationship to the church. "Husbands," he writes, "love your wives, as Christ loved the church and gave himself up for her, that he might sanctify her, having cleansed her by the washing of water with the word."

This indicates to me that baptism is not a magical rite. Being washed with the Word involves understanding the promise of God and being able to lay hold of it. Psalm 119:9 asks, "How can a young man cleanse his way?" and the answer is "by taking heed according to Your word" (NKJV). First Peter 1:23 speaks of the new birth in similar terms: "You have been born anew, not of perishable seed but of imperishable, through the living and abiding word of God"—through the cleansing that comes by the Scriptures.

But Jesus also said we must be born of the Spirit, and I think the story of the Incarnation helps us understand what this means. When the angel appeared to the virgin Mary and said, "Behold, you will conceive in your womb and bear a son, and you will call his name Jesus," [7] Mary asked how this was going to be, since she had no husband. The angel answered that the Holy Spirit would come upon her and the power of the Most High would overshadow her. Because of this, the child would be the Son of God.

The virgin birth is enshrined in our creed: "conceived by the Holy Spirit, born of the virgin Mary." We've believed it from the very beginning, but the church has never been able to explain it. It wasn't a sexual union, yet the Holy Spirit mysteriously and supernaturally planted the life of Jesus in the womb of a virgin. He did it; she didn't. He gave life; she received it. The Spirit began within her the life of the Son of God. That life was nurtured within her womb and eventually was born.

As amazing as it sounds, something like that has to happen to each of us when we're born again by the Spirit. The Spirit plants God's life inside us so that the life of God begins to grow within us. In Galatians 5 Paul says that the objective of the Spirit is that Christ be formed in us just as Jesus was formed in the womb of the virgin.

Where New Life Begins

A popular idea in our society is that everyone has a little spark of the divine within. But Scripture says that we're all dead in our trespasses and in sin until we're made alive by the Spirit. It's not a matter of fanning a sleeping spirit, but of new life being planted within.

The story of Nicodemus is so often misunderstood, I think, because a key verse is overlooked. It's verse 8: "The wind blows where it wills, and you hear the sound of it, but you do not know whence it comes or whither it goes; so it is with every one who is born of the Spirit."

In Greek, the word *pneuma*, used here, has a double, even triple, meaning. The same word can be translated *spirit* or *wind* or *breath*. The same three meanings apply to one Hebrew word, *ruach*, and one Latin word, *spiritus*. So this verse would be just as accurate if it were translated, "The Spirit blows where it wills and you hear the sound of it, but you do not know whence it comes or whither it goes; so it is with every one who is born of the wind."

Think of it. Those who are Christians, those who are born of the Spirit, who are believers in Christ, are "wind children." How does the wind work? You never know exactly where it's coming from or where it's going—but you *are* aware of its effects.

You can see it rustle the leaves. You can hear it whis-
tle around a corner. You can feel its refreshing coolness
on your cheek. If you've ever sat through a hurricane
or seen the path left by a tornado, you know how powerful the invisible force can be. As you see the wind's
effects, as you see the Spirit's effects, you conclude that
the wind or the Spirit is blowing—but you never conclude this because you've actually seen the wind or the
equally invisible Spirit.

Now here's the point: We can't give birth to
ourselves. When Jesus said, "You must be born again,"
was He telling Nicodemus to do something? No. Giving birth to yourself is impossible. We're saved by grace
through faith: "This is not your own doing; it is the
gift of God—not because of works, lest any man should
boast."[8]

If you're a believer, you're a miracle. The life of God
being planted in you is just as much a miracle as the
planting of the life of the Son of God in the womb of
the virgin Mary.

"But," you may say, "I've always thought that if
a person believes on the Lord Jesus Christ and accepts
Him as Savior, that person is born again."

That's right, but Paul says that no one can call Jesus
"Lord" except by the working of the Holy Spirit.[9]
Belief is the evidence of new birth; new birth is not the
evidence of belief. We can do nothing to earn salvation, for Jesus said that we don't seek Him; He seeks us.

Many Christians can name a certain day on which they
accepted Jesus Christ as their Savior. They say that was
the day they were born again. That may well be true,
and it may have been the day on which they first knew
they were able to confess their belief publicly. But every

woman who's had a child understands that life begins long before the moment of birth. In the same way, the day someone is born again is not the beginning of life; it's the end of a gestation that may have been going on for years. Adults know their physical birthdays because parents relay the information, not because of their own clear memory of the event.

Although God allows some people, like the apostle Paul, to have a dramatic conversion experience, He more often works gradually. As the parent, He knows when those people received the new life within them; they, like children, simply become more and more conscious of who they are. There's a point in a baby's life when he or she doesn't know the difference between the foot and the crib. Small babies can't distinguish themselves from their environments.

But finally the day comes when they realize that their foot is an ever-present part of their surroundings. Even later they discover that their foot is actually attached. Little by little an identity is built into a child and he or she begins to see self in reference to other people. Children eventually learn their own names and their parents' names. In a similar way, it can be years before a person knows he or she is a child of God and truly has a sense of Christian identity.

Our God, who won't make two snowflakes alike, wants to work in diverse ways. I know the day when I finally made my decision to follow Christ, but I've come to see that the Spirit of God was working in me years before that, getting me ready, overcoming my resistance, revealing to me the glory of the Son of God so that I would reach out to Him and take Him as my own Savior.

My parents were "godly" people. They knew the Lord; that was the most evident fact about them! The earliest memory I have is of the two people I regarded most highly on earth on their knees before One whom they regarded higher than themselves. They took it as their solemn responsibility to train their children in the Scriptures. We were required to memorize a new verse of Scripture every day—for fifteen years. We literally discussed Scriptures when we sat down, when we got up, when we went out and when we returned. They didn't much care whether we understood or not. Their philosophy was that hiding Scripture in our hearts would give the Holy Spirit something to work on in later years. It's not a popular child-rearing theory today, but it has its advantages!

The new birth is an invisible and often lengthy process that only God understands. As the rustle of the leaves is evidence of the wind, so belief in Jesus Christ is evidence that a person has entered the kingdom of God. Each of us knows within our own hearts whether or not we believe—even if a birthdate can't be named.

We can't give birth to ourselves spiritually. But neither can we just sit back and wait for the Spirit to plant His life within us—or within others. Just as physical conception involves the fusing of two elements, a sperm and an egg, so a physical conception involves the joining of the water or the Word and the Spirit.

Remember, Peter said we are born again by the Word of God, the cleansing agent. And when the Word and the Holy Spirit come together, the kingdom of God expands its sphere.

Over and over again in the Gospels, Jesus says, "He who has ears to hear, let him hear." He was aware that many people, maybe even most people, who hear the Word, who hear about the kingdom of God, don't understand it. Often, at the beginning of a church service, I pray that the Holy Spirit will make our ears to hear— that He will unclog our channels of understanding.

In Romans 10, the apostle Paul has a dialogue with himself. He says, "Every one who calls upon the name of the Lord will be saved." But then he asks several questions which build upon each other: How can you call if you've never heard? How can you hear unless someone tells you? How can someone tell you unless he's sent? Paul finally concludes that "faith comes from what is heard, and what is heard comes by the preaching of Christ" or by the preaching of the Word. He's pointing out the importance of a nurturing environment of faith, where the Word is spoken forth for the Spirit to quicken.

We're not able to control the movement of the wind— the Spirit—but we *are* able to place ourselves within hearing range of the cleansing Word, upon which the invisible Spirit can act to move us across that invisible line from unbelief to belief. And that is where life begins to make sense.

Part Two

The Self-Revelation of God

Chapter Three

Their Help in Ages Past

Before we go any further in our look at the working of the Holy Spirit in our lives, we must backtrack and see how He worked in the lives of people in the Old Testament. In many respects, the New Testament makes little sense apart from the Old. In fact, Jesus asked Nicodemus in that same conversation about the Spirit, "Are you a teacher of Israel and yet you do not understand this?"[1] Jesus' teaching about the invisible ways of the Spirit was nothing new.

Some time ago a parishioner commented that the Holy Spirit was born on Pentecost just as the incarnate Jesus was born on Christmas. I tried not to let my reaction show on my face, but I was horrified. The truth, you see, is that all three members of the Trinity are eternal. In fact, Genesis 1:2 says that "the earth was without form and void...and the Spirit of God was moving over the face of the waters." The Spirit was instrumental in creation and active throughout the years prior to Jesus' coming and Pentecost.

Yet the workings of the Holy Spirit throughout the Old Testament differ in several major ways from those in the New. So we need a clear understanding of both. The Old Testament is full of promises; the New Testament, of fulfillments. Those fulfillments are obviously difficult to understand unless we have a grasp of the promises behind them.

Together, the two testaments provide one continuous, unfolding story. This story is not of humanity's quest for God, but of God's self-revelation or self-disclosure to humanity—and that revelation is progressive. This means that recent generations have been shown things about the Lord that people born earlier did not know. Hebrews 1:1 summarizes it: "In many and various ways God spoke of old to our fathers by the prophets; but in these last days he has spoken to us by a Son." This verse from Hebrews describes two different ways of communication—two covenants. What we call the Old and New Testaments are more accurately called the Old and New Covenants. The first is an agreement God made with the descendants of Abraham; the second is an agreement He made with all of humankind. What do the agreements say? That God will be the God of certain people, that He will fashion a people as His namesake. And these people will be holy like Him.

God's holiness has always been a characteristic that distinguished Him from pagan gods. Zeus and Jupiter had great power, but they weren't considered holy. The Greek gods exhibited wisdom and beauty and strength, but not holiness.

In contrast, the holiness of the true God has been

evident since the beginning of time, when He first walked with Adam and Eve in the garden. And one of the wonders of God's human creation was the free will He placed within them so they could choose to walk in His holiness with Him. Adam and Eve were to exercise dominion over the created order, but the Lord said, "Of all the trees in the garden, you may freely eat except for the tree of the knowledge of good and evil. For the day you eat thereof you shall surely die."[2]

So Adam and Eve could choose to walk away from God as well. In light of that command, the critical question for them was, Under whose sovereignty will you live? The same question is ours as well. Who is going to be our God?

The Sovereignty of God

God, being God, had the right to set the rules of the universe He'd created. Part of the wonderful system He set up was giving that precious quality of freedom to those whom He had made in His image. But right away, at the very dawn of the human race, the freedom was exercised contrary to His purpose and holiness.

The closest Satan ever came to telling the truth was in the garden, when he said, "God knows that in the day that you eat thereof you shall become as God, knowing good and evil." He was right, of course. When they refused to obey the Lord and began to exercise their own will in opposition to His, they dethroned God and enthroned themselves in His place. They functioned as their own gods and became their own standard of right and wrong.

Remember what happened? The Lord came into the garden in the cool of the evening and said, "Adam, where are you?" Adam had hid himself because he felt afraid and ashamed before the eyes of a holy God. Adam and Eve had made pitiable little aprons of fig leaves, trying to appear shameless in the sight of God. But they were nevertheless naked. God knew it; they knew it; and their attempts to cover themselves were futile. With their initial acts of disobedience, Adam and Eve had chiseled an infinite chasm between humanity and God, whose holy nature required that His people be holy.

Part of God's ordering of creation demanded that blood be shed in order to cover sin from His sight. So even before Adam and Eve left the garden of Eden, God provided them with skins—of a dead, innocent animal— as coverings for their nakedness. Many generations later the Lord told the prophet Isaiah, "Your sin has built a wall of separation between me and you."[3] This is true of all Adam and Eve's descendants; but God, who is also a God of mercy and love, chose to make provision for sinful people who would respond to Him by faith. Scripture makes it abundantly clear that not every person is a child of God or a member of His family. Out of a rebellious human race, God is calling together a people who will be called by His name, and this calling forth is the subject of the Old and the New Covenants.

Jeremiah 31:31-33 is a pivotal passage that points us in two different directions. It looks back to describe the old agreement and looks forward to describe the new, which Jesus would usher in when He came to earth about five hundred years after Jeremiah's death:

"Behold the days are coming, says the Lord, when I will make a new covenant with the house of Israel and the house of Judah, not like the covenant which I made with their fathers when I took them by the hand to bring them out of the land of Egypt, my covenant which they broke, though I was their husband, says the Lord. But this is the covenant which I will make with the house of Israel after those days, says the Lord: I will put my law within them, and I will write it upon their hearts; and I will be their God, and they shall be my people."

This passage gives us a great deal of information. First, it says that it is the Lord who is the initiator of the covenant. Abraham, to whom the Old Covenant was first given, didn't one day just sidle up to the Almighty and say, "Let's get together on this." All the way through Scripture one thing is constant: God acts and we respond. We see that truth clearly here, where He promises, "I will make a new covenant, not like the old covenant which they broke."

The New Testament book of Hebrews tells us that if the Old Covenant had worked, there wouldn't have been any need for a new one.[4] But why didn't it work? What about our human nature made it fail?

The Abrahamic Covenant

The original Abrahamic covenant is recorded in Genesis 12:1-3:

"Now the Lord said to Abram, 'Go from your country and your kindred and your father's house to the land that I will show you. And I will make of you a great nation, and I will bless you, and make your name great, so that you will be a blessing. I will bless those who bless you, and him who curses you I will curse; and by you all the families of the earth shall bless themselves.' "

Abram was a Chaldean. For some reason unknown to us, God chose to reveal Himself to this one man and tell him to pack his bags and move to a new place. In response, Abram left, dependent on God's promise of blessing.

Genesis 17:1-7 gives more details of the covenant: "When Abram was ninety-nine years old the Lord appeared to Abram, and said to him, 'I am God Almighty; walk before me, and be blameless. And I will make my covenant between me and you, and will multiply you exceedingly.' Then Abram fell on his face; and God said to him, 'Behold, my covenant is with you, and you shall be the father of a multitude of nations. No longer shall your name be Abram, but your name shall be Abraham; for I have made you the father of a multitude of nations. I will make you exceedingly fruitful; and I will make nations of you, and kings shall come forth from you. And I will establish my covenant between me and you and your descendants after you throughout their generations for an everlasting covenant, to be God to you and to your descendants after you.' "

Here God said, "I will be the God of you and your descendants; you will be my people." There is no *if* condition in this passage, but God did expect Abraham to "walk before him and be blameless." And God would test Abraham's faithfulness. Later, when Isaac— Abraham and Sarah's only son, and the descendant through whom God had promised His blessing—was an adolescent, God would say, "Abraham, take your son, your only son Isaac, whom you love, and go to the land of Moriah and offer him there as a burnt offering."

I can only imagine Abraham's response when he heard that command: "But, Lord, You promised to give me a posterity like the sands of the sea through this child— and now You're telling me to slay him? Lord...."

But Abraham obeyed. Ever since Adam and Eve had

left the garden, people who walked with God had been offering Him sacrifices. Abel and Noah are specifically mentioned as offerers of sacrifice, and Abraham had sacrificed before this trip. So he knew what God wanted, and no doubt Isaac knew what a sacrifice was as well. On the way up the mountain the boy turned to his dad and said, "We have the fire and the wood, but where is the sacrifice?" Abraham answered simply, "The Lord will provide Himself a sacrifice. Keep walking."

When they reached the top of the summit, they built an altar. Then Abraham bound Isaac's hands and feet, laid him on the altar and actually drew the knife. But the Lord intervened and said, "Stop. Don't touch that child. I never intended you to kill him. I just wanted to see if you would obey Me. I wanted to know if you were sure I would keep My promise."[5] The book of Hebrews says that Abraham was so filled with faith that he believed God would have kept His promise, even if it meant raising the child from the dead.[6]

The story ends with Abraham looking up and seeing a ram caught by his horns in a nearby thicket. God had provided a sacrifice for that occasion, and because Abraham had proved faithful, God repeated His promise to bless Abraham's descendants, and to make them numberless like the stars in the sky.

The People of God

The Lord renewed the Abrahamic covenant with Abraham's son, Isaac, and with Isaac's son Jacob. But then the Scriptures are silent for several generations, until God spoke to Moses, some six hundred years after God had revealed Himself to Abraham. The children of Israel, or Abraham's descendants, had been enslaved by the Egyptian pharaoh. God, through Moses, had led them out of captivity and into the desert, which they had to cross before they could get back to Israel, the land God had promised to Abraham.

God was with His people as they journeyed. They could easily see that this was true, because "the Lord went before them by day in a pillar of cloud to lead them...and by night in a pillar of fire to give them light."[7]

Nehemiah 9:19-20 also records that the Spirit of God was with the children of Israel: "Thou in thy great mercies didst not forsake them in the wilderness, the pillar of cloud which led them in the way did not depart from them by day, nor the pillar of fire by night by which they should go. Thou gavest *thy good Spirit* to instruct them, and didst not withhold manna from their mouth, and gavest them water for their thirst."

After they had entered the desert, God added some fine print to the Abrahamic covenant. He inserted some if-you-do-this-then-I-will-do-that conditions which clearly show the human part in the agreement.

In Exodus 34:27, the Lord says to Moses, "Write these words; in accordance with these words I have made a covenant with you and with Israel." The words God gave Moses were the Ten Commandments which summarized His will for His peoople. God no longer said, "I will bless the descendants of Abraham, no-strings-attached"; instead, He said He would do this if they kept or obeyed the words of His commandments. The children of Israel at first responded positively. When Moses came down from the mountain, the people "signed on the dotted line." They said, "Yes, we will obey. We accept this covenant." But God told Moses that He knew and saw the fallibility in people's hearts. He said, "I have heard the words of this people....Oh, that they had such a mind as this always, to fear me and to keep all my commandments, that it might go well with them and with their children for ever!"[8] You can almost hear a sigh in the heart of the Lord. He heard them saying, "Yes, we will obey," and He wished they would only continue to keep their word.

But they didn't. Again and again they broke the law God had placed over their heads. So instead of receiving the blessing He had promised, they suffered under the contrasting curse.

Again, Nehemiah records: "Many years thou didst bear with them, and didst warn them *by thy Spirit through thy prophets*, but they would not give ear. Therefore, thou didst give them into the hands of the peoples of the land. Nevertheless, in thy great mercies thou didst not make an end of them or forsake them, for thou art a gracious and merciful God."[9]

Blessings and Curses

It's hard for some people to understand how God can speak of curses. But that's the way a loving yet holy God set the universe in motion. The pattern started in the garden of Eden. If there is such a thing as truth, there is automatically such a thing as error. (Conversely, error can't exist if truth doesn't.) The word *up* would make no sense if there weren't a corresponding *down*. The Scriptures tell us that the Lord, in giving the commandments, was establishing a specific measure of right, the opposite of which would be wrong. And if obedience to His standard brings blessings, disobedience brings calamity. He's not a vengeful God, but because He has established truth, these things will always cut both ways.

In Deuteronomy 28, the Lord goes on at great length

about the bountiful blessings and disastrous judgments tied to keeping or breaking His rules. These rules are summarized in what we call the Ten Commandments, but here they're ponderously spelled out in 613 you-must and you-must-not laws. Two of His images are graphic opposites: If the people obey, the Lord will make them to be "the head, and not the tail"; He will make them "tend upward only, and not downward." If the people disobey, the images reverse.

In a very real sense, the children of Israel were made slaves of God's law. They were under the rule of these external commands written on stone tablets. The law was a master that told them what they had to do at all times.

Nevertheless, the Old Covenant, the Law, failed—not because there was something wrong with the Law, but because there was something wrong with human nature. No one reacts well to being told what he or she must do, and although the Law was intended to produce righteousness, it produced greater sin. Even so, the holy yet loving Lord again made provision to cover the sins of His people—if they repented.

Repentance Through Sacrifice

Right after He gave Moses the Ten Commandments, God gave directions for how the people were to build a tabernacle in which He would reside. They were to construct a tent with two parts: the Holy Place and an inner Holy of Holies, separated from each other by a thick curtain. The ark of the covenant, the dwelling place of God, was to be placed in the Holy of Holies. No one was to enter this section except for the high priest; and he could enter only once a year, after he had made a sacrifice for himself. This took place on the Day of

Atonement or what we know as Yom Kippur. Leviticus 16 describes what happened: The high priest cast lots over two goats. One was killed and offered as a burnt offering unto the Lord, for Scripture says, "Without the shedding of blood there is no forgiveness of sins."[10] Death was required, but something else as well. The priest then laid his hands on the second goat, the goat of Azazel, which means wilderness, and he confessed aloud the sins of the people. Then this live goat was set loose to wander away across the wilderness and out of sight. The children of Israel could see the symbolism: Their sins had been borne away by a scapegoat. (This is, by the way, the origin of that word.)

Yet even right after this atonement, a penitent Jew could not go into the Holy of Holies. A mediator or a go-between, a high priest, always stood between God and the children who were called by His name. Why? Although the sacrifice and the scapegoat sent the sins of the people to the desert and restored their place as the people of God, no animal sacrifice was able to restore them to the perfect holy-to-holy relationship Adam had once had with God. The Old Testament sacrifices could *cover* sins or send them out of sight into the wilderness, but they couldn't actually remove the people's sin. For that kind of deliverance from sin and the Law that seemed to make them repeatedly rebel, the children of Israel looked into the future, to the coming of One who would bring in the New Covenant.

The Old Covenant was still in effect centuries later when Jeremiah contrasted the heavy Law with the coming New Covenant. Jeremiah was especially aware of the consequences of disobedience, for during his lifetime the Babylonians utterly devastated God's people. They destroyed Jerusalem, which had been the capital city since the days of King David. They destroyed Solomon's temple, legendary for its beauty. Everything that had seemed important to Jeremiah lay in ruins before him, yet his faith in God did not waver; he clearly saw that the destruction was God's judgment against His rebellious people.

Jeremiah had prophesied that this would happen, so when calamity did strike, he knew it was not the "end of the world." Instead, he realized that a day was coming when God would do a new thing, institute a new covenant that would change how He dealt with people whom He called His own.

Upon, Within

In the next chapter we'll talk more about God's institution of the New Covenant and what that means for us. But before we do, let's look at a major difference between how the Holy Spirit worked among men and women before the coming of Christ, and how He works after the Lord's first coming. I can't emphasize enough how separated God was from His people during the Old Testament generations. The dwelling place of the Lord was so set apart that anyone who touched the ark of the covenant would die. This was no idle threat; Uzzah, a man who in the reign of King David reached out to steady the ark which was being transported, was stricken dead. Although God dramatically made His presence known among His people, He was a very "other," external being.

Before the death and resurrection of Jesus, God dealt with the people whom He called by His name, but He didn't dwell within them. For centuries, God's law was written on stones, not on people's hearts. Throughout these Old Testament years, however, the Holy Spirit seems to have come temporarily upon certain specified individuals to give them a special, needed anointing of power. It happened over and over again—with prophets, priests, kings and other leaders.

In Jewish ritual, this anointing of the Holy Spirit was symbolized by an agent of God taking a little oil and pouring it on a person's forehead. The anointing was for a specific task or duty, sort of a "little-dab-will-do-you" application. When Samuel anointed Saul with oil, for example, indicating that God had chosen Saul to be Israel's first king, Samuel said, "The Spirit of the Lord will come mightily upon you, and you shall prophesy."[11]

Some of the most dramatic anointings of the Holy Spirit were of military leaders, and their stories are found in the Book of Judges. This book covers a period of history shortly after the death of Moses and his successor, Joshua. The children of Israel, now in the Promised Land, had begun to fall away from the commands of the Lord. A cycle—of disobedience, punishment or enslavement, repentance, and deliverance—repeats fifteen times during the Book of Judges. In story after story, the Spirit of God comes upon an individual who leads the country to God's freedom. Chapter 3, verse 10, says, "The Spirit of the Lord came upon him [Othniel], and he judged Israel; he went out to war..."; 11:29 says, "The Spirit of the Lord came upon Jephthah"; 14:19 and 15:14 say, "And the Spirit of the Lord came mightily upon him [Samson]." Each of these people had specific tasks for which they were temporarily and externally empowered. As long as each judge lived, God's people followed His ways. But sadly enough, when each judge died, the Israelites turned their backs on God.

Alongside Old Testament promises for a New Covenant are promises for a coming Anointed One, whom the Holy Spirit would empower to deliver God's people from oppression—once and for all. The Hebrew word "Messiah" and the Greek word "Christ" both mean "Anointed One"—the One upon whom the Spirit would rest so as to break all bonds of captivity. Isaiah 11:1 says: "There shall come forth a shoot from the stump of Jesse, and a branch shall grow out of his roots. And the Spirit of the Lord shall rest upon him, the spirit of wisdom and understanding, the spirit of counsel and might, the spirit of knowledge and of the fear of the Lord." Isaiah 42:1-2 makes another reference to the coming Anointed One: "Behold my servant, whom I uphold, my chosen, in whom my soul delights; I have put my Spirit upon him, and he will bring forth justice to the nations."

The ordinary Jewish layperson expected God's power to come upon this Anointed One to bring political deliverance, as had previous anointed ones. As it turned out, however, the Messiah's salvation was not "of this world." Rather it ushered in a new spiritual age, the New Covenant, which provided humankind with a clearer revelation of who God was.

Yet another Old Testament prophecy referred to a future day when the Holy Spirit would come upon anyone—not just a chosen few who were specially called forth as leaders. Joel 2:28 says, "And it shall come to pass afterward, that I will pour out my Spirit on all flesh." How the prophets of those days, who so clearly discerned the voice of God, must have groaned with impatience—to know that God had promised a time would come when He would send His Spirit to write His law *within* His people's hearts, not just on tablets of stone, and to settle *upon* them with His power.

Chapter Four

Our Hope
for Years to Come

When God saw that the time had come to reveal more of Himself to humankind, He came to earth. Galatians 4:4-5 says: "But when the time had fully come, God sent forth His Son, born of woman, born under the law, to redeem those who were under the law, so that we might receive adoption as sons."

J.B. Phillips has used a wonderful phrase to describe this relatively small and insignificant part of the universe: "the visited planet." God, the creator and sustainer of solar systems and galaxies, became flesh and dwelt among us. In the human form of Jesus of Nazareth, God was physically born of a woman, born under the Old Covenant, and He lived in Palestine for thirty-three years.

Because Jesus was God made flesh, because He was conceived by the Holy Spirit, the Holy Spirit was always within Him, despite His birth under the Old Covenant.

But something happened to Him at the age of thirty. Jesus went at that time to the edge of the Jordan River, where His cousin John was teaching and baptizing. Though He was sinless and had no need for the purifying rite, Jesus asked John to baptize Him. Then, when the Lord came up out of the water, the Spirit of God descended upon Him in the form of a dove.

Several years later, when Peter was explaining the gospel to the Gentile Cornelius, Peter specifically mentioned Jesus' baptism: "He was anointed with the Holy Spirit and with power."[1] On this day, the Messiah-designate became *the* Messiah. At this moment, He turned away from the carpenter's bench and began His public ministry, the task for which He had come into the world.

This empowering gives us a clue about why the people of Nazareth, Jesus' childhood neighbors, seemed puzzled at what had become of the boy down the street. Nazareth wasn't—and still isn't—much of a town. For thirty years Jesus had lived there without making any ripples. Then He went off and started preaching—drawing great crowds—and miraculously healing people. When He came back to town, they asked, "Where did this man get this wisdom and these mighty works? Is not this the carpenter's son? Is not His mother called Mary?"[2] He didn't seem much different from any other local boy—until this day when the Holy Spirit came *upon* Him with power, after which He "went about doing good and healing all that were oppressed by the devil, for God was with him."[3]

How did Jesus usher in the New Covenant? By being the righteousness that stands between God's fallen people and His holy presence; by being the drawbridge that allows God, in the person of the Holy Spirit, to walk into and reside within the hearts of those who look to Him, in faith, as their redemption.

The Purpose for Which He'd Come

Throughout His ministry, Jesus knew the purpose for which He'd come; He knew that He was to be the perfect Lamb whose death would actually take away—remove—the sin of the people who were called by God's name. He knew the Old Testament prophecies that He would fulfill, such as Isaiah 53:5 and 10:

"He was wounded for our transgressions, he was bruised for our iniquities; upon him was the chastisement that made us whole, and with his stripes we are healed.... Yet it was the will of the Lord to bruise him; he has put him to grief; when he makes himself an offering for sin...."

Some years ago I met a young, devout Orthodox Jew from the Bronx on a plane heading for Israel. I chatted with him on the trip over and—when we arrived in Jerusalem just before sundown on Friday evening, which marked the beginning of his sabbath—I offered to take him to the Western Wall. Whenever I go to that site I stand back in awe of the scene before me. You can hear the lament of the people praying that God will lift the reproach of His people. This particular evening I silently waited a long time while this man prayed, but finally I picked up on a conversation we had started in the plane. "Tell me," I said, "what do you think of Jesus Christ?"

As I suspected, he had a strong opinion and answered, "I think he got exactly what he deserved. He claimed to be God. He said, 'He that hath seen me hath seen the Father....I and My Father are one.' He presumed

57

to forgive people's sins. I know you Christians think we Jews crucified Jesus, but I think God put Him there as punishment for His blasphemy."

Although this young man's reasoning was wrong (yet predictable, as Isaiah 53 also says that Jesus would be esteemed "stricken, smitten by God"), he was exactly right in saying that God put Jesus on the cross. It was planned for one purpose: 1 John 3:8 says, "The reason the Son of God appeared was to destroy the works of the devil."

Jesus knew that those thousands of bulls and goats and lambs sacrificed over the centuries had not atoned for a single sin. The sacrifices and the Yom Kippur ceremony had been an elaborate preparation so that the people could grasp the idea that someone innocent had to die in behalf of the guilty.

In God's plan, no one else but Jesus could successfully do it. The atoner had to be God, because He was the offended One. Yet he also had to be a human, because humankind had been the offender. The only solution was for the penalty to be paid by the God-man, Jesus. He's called the "Lamb of God who takes away the sin of the world"[4] because when He hung upon the cross, the sin of the whole world was placed upon Him.

In fact, 2 Corinthians 5:21 makes an even stronger statement: "For our sake"—for your sake and for my sake—"he [God] made him [Jesus] to be sin who knew no sin, so that in him we might become the righteousness of God." In commenting on this passage, Martin Luther pointed out that in that dreadful moment when Jesus hung on the cross, it wasn't that Jesus became a sinner in the sight of God; it was that He became sin. All of the evil of the world was placed upon Him. And because

He died in *our* place, *we* can become the righteousness of God. Imagine a courtroom scene with a judge and a jury, and with yourself as the defendant. Witness after witness takes the stand and describes all the sinful things you have done. You hang your head in shame because you're obviously guilty. The jury leaves and in no time returns with a guilty verdict. The judge pronounces the death sentence. John 5:22 says that God ''has given all judgment to the Son.'' So Jesus, your judge, comes down off the bench, puts His arm around you and says, ''I will go to the electric chair in your place. Although you are guilty, you are acquitted before God and righteous in His sight.''

Jesus' death brings together the various threads that run through the Old Testament story. On the cross, right before He died, Jesus said, ''It is finished.''[5] That was no cry of defeat and despair, but a ringing declaration—telling heaven and hell that He had accomplished everything He had come to do. Satan, sin and death were conquered; the ultimate atoning sacrifice for sin had been made. Of course, people still die and people still sin, but death and sin and the devil no longer have the last word. They've been bound up so that they're powerless.

Jesus knew the work He had come to do was complete. Sin had been paid for and the channel had been opened so humanity could be redeemed and restored to its holy God. Matthew 27:50-51 gives us an important piece of information with regard to this truth: ''And Jesus cried again with a loud voice and yielded up his spirit. And behold, the curtain of the temple was torn in two, from top to bottom.'' As of that moment, humankind could walk into the presence of God—without the fear of being struck dead, without the mediation of a priest. Why? Because now, as much of the book of Hebrews explains, Jesus—God Himself—is our high priest. As 1 Timothy 2:5 says, "There is one mediator between God and men, the man Christ Jesus, who gave himself as a ransom for all."

Not only were the old sacrificial and mediation systems put to rest, but the Old Covenant was here replaced with the New. On the night of the Last Supper, Jesus spoke of His death: "This is my blood of the [new] covenant, which is poured out for many."[6] When Jesus asked us to celebrate the Last Supper, He wanted us to be reminded that we are people of the New Covenant, not the Old. Romans 10:4 says, "For Christ is the end of the law that every one who has faith may be justified."

Changed From the Inside Out

The two covenants display a major difference: The Law, which was once an external master towering over the heads of God's people, is now written within their hearts. Even though the same rights and wrongs are God's standard, the pressure to obey them is internal. We're changed from the inside out. There's a big difference between being told you *have* to do something and doing something because you *want* to do it.

As a parent I've often thought how wonderful it would be if I could somehow get inside the head or heart of my children so I could make them understand and want to do what they should. The Old Covenant, which God's people served as slaves, said, "You've got to do this whether you want to or not—or else." But the new way establishes internal motivation or direction, with the Law planted in the hearts of those who believe.

Ezekiel graphically compares the Old and New

Covenants: "A new heart I will give you, and a new spirit I will put within you; and I will take out of your flesh the heart of stone and give you a heart of flesh.... And I will put my spirit within you, and cause you to walk in my statutes and be careful to observe my ordinances. You shall dwell in the land which I gave to your fathers; and you shall be my people, and I will be your God."[7]

Adoption, Reception

What does the New Covenant actually mean for us, God's people? Above all, it means that the Holy Spirit is actually within us. I like to paraphrase Ezekiel's words by saying that God, under the New Covenant, performs heart transplants. He wants to take out hearts that are hardened and resistant to His will, and replace them with hearts that are repentant and open and responsive to Him. He wants to usher people into His kingdom and call them adopted children.

Remember Galatians 4:4-5, which says that "God sent forth his Son...so that we might receive adoption as sons"? This verse reflects a peculiarity about first-century Roman law: An adopted child could never be disowned or disinherited. If a natural-born child sufficiently infuriated a father, the father could cut the child off; but a child who was chosen to be a member of the family could never be repudiated. In Psalm 51 David prayed that God would not take His Spirit away from him, but David made that request because he was under the Old Covenant. We, who are adopted children, need have *no* fear of that happening.

The Galatians passage goes on to say: "And because you are sons, God has sent the Spirit of his Son into our hearts, crying, 'Abba! Father!' So through God you are no longer a slave but a son."[8] Because we are God's children, the Holy Spirit, the Spirit of Jesus, resides within us and cries, "Daddy, Daddy!" like a child who runs with open arms toward a father and is picked up in his arms. That's the family spirit, and that's what we were given on the third day after Jesus' crucifixion.

Because Jesus was God, death could not hold Him captive. On the morning of the third day after His death, He rose from the grave, having battled and defeated humankind's ultimate curse. John 20:19-22 says:

"On the evening of that day...Jesus came and stood among [the disciples] and said to them, 'Peace be with you.' When he had said this, he showed them his hands and his side....And Jesus said to them again, 'Peace be with you. As the Father has sent me, even so send I you.' And when he had said this, he breathed on them and said to them, 'Receive the Holy Spirit.' "

Here the life of God is bestowed through the breath— or wind or spirit—of God. Remember, in Greek and in Hebrew the same word has all three meanings. A similar transfusion of life took place in the very creation of man, as "God breathed into (Adam) the breath of life and he became a living soul."[9] The dead, dry bones that Ezekiel saw in the valley were also brought to life by the breath of God.[10] And here again, on the evening of Resurrection Day, God breathed life. At this moment, the disciples became Christians, indwelt by the Spirit, the giver of life.

This indwelling is referred to again and again in the New Testament, and nowhere more literally than in 1 Corinthians, where Paul twice refers to us Christians as God's temples: "Do you not know that you are God's temple and that God's Spirit dwells in you? If any one destroys God's temple, God will destroy him. For God's temple is holy, and that temple you are."[11] Then three chapters later he repeats himself: "Do you not know that your body is a temple of the Holy Spirit within you, which you have from God? You are not your own; you were bought with a price. So glorify God in your body."[12] What a difference between this temple of God and the Holy of Holies in the tabernacle!

I used to subscribe to what I called "the pot theory." I imagined Christians as clay vessels, and I claimed that some "pots" were filled with a little bit of the Holy Spirit, while others were filled with a bit more. Perhaps some were half full; some were three-quarters full; a few were full to the top.

But as I studied further, I came to a more clear understanding of John 3:34, where Jesus says that God does not give His Spirit by measure. Romans 8:9 says that every Christian has the Holy Spirit, so if a person is a Christian, even an infant Christian, he or she has received the Holy Spirit in His fullness. That person is full to the brim, as were the disciples on Easter evening (see John 20:22).

Part Three

The Spirit Within You

Chapter Five

The Spirit of Truth

The night before Jesus was crucified, He talked to His disciples at length, preparing them for the events that would soon change the very fabric of their lives. Three of the Gospel writers describe the dinner portion of this evening, known as "The Lord's Supper," at which Jesus referred to the bread and the wine as His broken body and spilt blood. This was the institution of the New Covenant.

In the fourth Gospel, however, John doesn't mention the supper. Instead, he details a lengthy discourse which includes Jesus' most complete teaching on the Holy Spirit. At one point in this discourse, Jesus says something that must have seemed outlandish: "It is to your advantage that I go away."[1]

John doesn't describe here his own reaction or that of the other disciples, but let's just imagine it for a moment. I know that if I'd been one of the disciples, I would have jumped in and said, "But, Master, how in the world can you say that? We've just started to find out who you really are. We've just started to believe in you. There's so much we have to learn. We love you. We need you here. It can't possibly be to our advantage for you to leave."

In the previous verse John says that Jesus knew the disciples' sorrow, yet He went right on with His explanation: "It's to your advantage that I go away, for if I don't go away, the Counselor will not come. But if I go away, I'll send him unto you."

Jesus had been the disciples' continual companion for three and a half years. He and this little band of men had lived together, eaten together, ministered together. These twelve had received His private teaching; they had seen His miracles. In short, Jesus had been their constant counselor, and this should come as no surprise; the prophet Isaiah, 750 years before, had in fact foretold this characteristic of the coming Messiah: "For to us a child is born, to us a son is given; and the government will be upon his shoulder, and his name will be called 'Wonderful Counselor, Mighty God, Everlasting Father, Prince of Peace.' "[2]

Now most of what Isaiah prophesied in that passage is hardly unusual. Children are born every minute of the day, and nearly half of those children are sons. Even the Messiah's having the government on His shoulders is hardly amazing; heirs to thrones are born into every generation. But the rest of this verse—"Wonderful Counselor, Mighty God, Everlasting Father, Prince of Peace"—pointed to someone who was truly unique.

Most people hear this verse sung in Handel's "Messiah", and because of a dramatic pause in the score, it's natural to think there's a comma between *wonderful* and *counselor*. Actually, the King James Version of the text does have a comma, but it shouldn't be there. The Messiah is a wonderful Counselor and a mighty God. Isaiah said that Jesus was to be known as the most proficient of counselors.

The Greek word in John 16:7 translated as "Counselor" in the Revised Standard Version is *paraclete*, which means "someone brought alongside to help." The King James Version uses the word *Comforter*; the New American Standard Bible says *Helper*; the Jerusalem Bible says *Advocate*. All of those English words taken together help give us a more complete idea of who Jesus was to His disciples.

The word "mentor" is a popular term today for the kind of role Jesus played in the lives of the disciples. Sometimes they would ask His advice. I can just imagine hot-tempered Peter, for example, getting into an argument with someone, cooling down a few hours later, and then going to Jesus for His opinion on the matter. At the same time the Lord was a powerful role model. The disciples would silently watch Him in action and visually take in His counsel.

But now Jesus was saying that He was going away. In John 14:16, just a few minutes earlier, He had said, "I will pray the Father, and he will give you another Counselor, to be with you for ever, even the Spirit of truth, whom the world cannot receive, because it neither sees him nor knows him; *you know him, for he dwells with you, and will be in you.*"

Jesus spoke here with authority—more authority than I would have, I'm sure. I might have said something like, "I will pray the Father, and *perhaps* He will give

you another counselor," or "I will pray the Father, and
trust He will give another." But Jesus seems to have
had no doubt that what He was asking the Father would
give. What gave Him that confidence? Not some supernatural knowledge, but rather His natural knowledge
of the Old Testament promises of the New Covenant.
You see, although He was the Son of God, Jesus was
human in every respect—except that He never sinned.
He "emptied himself...being born in the likeness of
men."[3] Part of what that means is that He closed off
any privileged knowledge He had of the will of the
Father. He learned the Father's will exactly the same
way you and I do—through observation, through teaching, through sifting out the facts. In those days,
everybody thought the world was flat, and I suspect that
Jesus thought so, too. Why? Because He wasn't God
just "dressed up" as if He were a man. Very early in
church history that idea was condemned as heresy. In
Jesus, God really became human and laid aside, not His
deity, but the prerogatives, splendor and glory of His
deity. Because of that, He came to a knowledge of the
will of the Father through the Word and through the
working of the Holy Spirit who illumined Him. Because
He was yielded and open to the Father and desired only
the Father's will, the light of God constantly flowed into
Him.

Continual, Continuous

As a man, Jesus was physically limited like any
human. That means He had a body like ours that is
bound within time and space. My schedule sometimes
demands that I be in several cities in the course of one
day. Now it's possible for me to address two groups,
back to back. It's even possible for me to be videotaped

and be seen simultaneously by many groups. But it's quite impossible for me to stand behind a lectern in Washington at the same time I'm standing behind a pulpit in Darien, Connecticut.

The same was true of Jesus in His incarnate state. If He came to your church to speak to you on a Sunday morning, you would receive His counsel, but then you would go home to your house and He would go home to His. He would no longer be with you.

When Jesus arrived in Bethany too late for Lazarus' funeral, Martha exclaimed, "Oh, if You'd only been here, You could have kept my brother from dying."[4] Jesus hadn't been there because He was somewhere else, and He couldn't be in two places at once.

If you check your dictionary, you'll notice a slight but important (and often overlooked) difference between the words *continual* and *continuous*. "Continual" means "recurring again and again; repeated often." "Continuous" means "going on or extending without interruption or break."

When Jesus walked on the earth, He was the disciples' *continual* counselor and companion. Their times together were frequent and repeated, but intermittent. Jesus sometimes left them to go pray. If He was having a quiet, private conversation with Peter, He was not simultaneously "with" John and Andrew, who may have been walking on ahead, already having turned the next bend in the road. It was physically impossible for Jesus to be their *continuous* counselor, as constant and present as a perfectly functioning heart.

Now imagine for a moment having Jesus as your *continuous* companion, closer than a spouse. When you wake up in the morning, He's sitting on the end of the bed, ready to talk with you about plans for the day ahead. Together, you can discuss major problems as well as minor irritations. When you go downstairs, turn on the stove and walk away for a minute, you hear Him say, "The eggs are burning," even before you smell them. When you go over to check on them, you see that His counsel has been right. At every turn He's present. Although Jesus was never able to be this constant with any one of His disciples, this presence—and more—is what He was promising when He told them, "It's to your advantage that I go away."

The coming of the Holy Spirit would make Jesus accessible to all of us at all times. The disciples had no idea how important this internal presence would be to them in time: Within just a few years of this conversation, they would be scattered because of persecution. If the man Jesus had been with Thomas in India, He wouldn't have been with Peter in Palestine, and if He'd been with Peter, He wouldn't have been with Paul in Turkey or Mark in Africa.

The Mind of Christ

In each person's mind is a private little sanctuary into which no one can enter. Not a soul on the face of the earth knows exactly what you're thinking at any given moment. I may often *think* I know what thoughts are running through my wife's head, but she tells me I'm not always right. Paul expresses this reality perfectly in 1 Corinthians 2:11: "For what person knows a man's thoughts except the spirit of the man which is in him?" And he continues, "So also no one comprehends the thoughts of God except the Spirit of God."

What's he saying? No one can figure out what God is up to by studying the stars or gazing at his or her navel or looking into a crystal ball. No one knows the purposes, the will, the plan of God except the Spirit of God—the very same Spirit of God who moved upon the prophets of old to enable them to write the Scriptures, the very same Spirit of God who is within a believer. Too often we think of the Holy Spirit as some vague force just floating around in the air somewhere, and forget that *we* are His temples! Paul continues in his letter to the Corinthians, "Now we have received not the spirit of the world, but the Spirit which is from God, that we might understand." The Spirit—the Counselor within you—knows the will of God about everything that concerns you. He is not mystified by the issues that mystify you. He has no fear of the future or questions about how things are going to turn out.

The Spirit has been given this information, and He's been given to you so that He might lead you into the truth of God's will. First Corinthians 2 ends with a wonderful summary sentence: "We have the mind of Christ." But what is the mind of Christ?

John 14 gives us some clues in this regard, because it says a great deal about who Jesus is and who the Spirit is. In verse 6 Jesus says, "I am the way, the truth, and the life." In verse 16 He says that the Holy Spirit is the "Spirit of truth." In Greek, the word for "truth"—*aletheia*—is a picture word. It's made up of the prefix "a" and the noun *letheia. Letheia* means *veil*—a tangible veil, such as a woman would wear over her face. The prefix "a" makes the word negative, designating its opposite. An example of how this prefix works is our word *atheist.* A "theist" is a believer in God; an "atheist" is a nonbeliever in God. The same is true of the word *agnostic. Gnosis* is the Greek word for knowledge, and an "agnostic" is one who claims not to know. The Greek word for truth, *aletheia*, literally means, then, "without a veil." When Jesus said, "I am the truth," He was saying that truth, at its root, isn't a doctrine or an idea or a teaching or a principle or a philosophy. It's a living person. He was saying, in effect, "When you look at me you are seeing truth—God Himself—unveiled." That's why Jesus, in verse 9 of this chapter, could also say, "He who has seen me has seen the Father."

Right here in John 14 we have a clear picture of the Trinity. Although we must distinguish among the Father, the Son and the Spirit—the Father is not the Son nor is the Son the Holy Spirit nor is the Spirit the Father—the three persons are one God, not three gods.

A basic tenet of the Jewish law and of the Christian faith is that "the Lord our God is one Lord"[5]; yet this one God has revealed Himself as Father, Son and Holy Spirit. John 1:18 says that the Son shows us who the Father is ("No one has ever seen God; the only Son, who is in the bosom of the Father, he has made him known") and John 15:14-15 says that the Spirit will show us who Jesus, the truth, is ("[The Spirit] will glorify [the Son], for he will take what is mine and declare it to you. All that the Father has is mine; therefore I said that [the Spirit] will take what is mine and declare it to you"). This Last Supper discourse also says that the Spirit is sent to us by both the Son and the Father.[6] The Holy Spirit is simply God made present to us now, in this age.

If Jesus is truth and the Holy Spirit is the Spirit of truth, it's Jesus' Spirit that lives within us; it's His mind that is ours. Galatians 4:6 in fact calls the Holy Spirit the Spirit of Jesus, and the last sentence of Jesus recorded by Matthew is "Lo, I am with you always." Because Jesus and the Spirit are two forms of the same truth, Jesus can say, "I'm going away" and "I am with you," without contradicting Himself. I truly believe that our relationship with Jesus in the form of His Spirit is even more intimate than the one the disciples had with Jesus the man.

The Counselor

One common problem in counseling is that different approaches work with different people. Only the Lord God knows what's in a person's heart or mind, and I've never found that people conform to any set patterns, other than that they all sin. For some, a form of Christian behavioral modification may be the answer—having them conform to scriptural mandates. For another, the personal approach of one-on-one prayer for inner healing may be the key. The danger lies in insisting that a certain approach is the answer for all. The only answer for all is Jesus, but we all come to knowledge of Him and healing through Him in different ways. "Buying into a system" tends to add to or compound the problems rather than aid or cure them. But the Holy Spirit can work through any problem brought to Him, and much more quickly than a human counselor can. Human counselors will always falter somewhere along the line, and bitter feelings can result. I've often told my congregation that I'm not a counselor—and that's because I know *the Counselor* is the only solution. I much prefer the method Francis and Judith MacNutt use in their times of prayer ministry: just praying in the Spirit for a person, allowing the Spirit of truth to reach deep within and do the work that only He can do.

John quotes Jesus as saying, "But the Counselor, the Holy Spirit, whom the Father will send in my name, he will teach you all things, and bring to your remembrance all that I have said to you,"[7] and "When the Spirit of truth comes, he will guide you into all the truth."[8] I'm so glad that the Spirit of Jesus is both the Counselor *and* the Spirit of truth. All of us have probably received bad advice before, based on wrong information or judgment; and if a certain person repeatedly gives us bad advice, our trust in that person as an advisor plummets. But our Counselor is Himself truth, and so He is utterly trustworthy.

As truth, one of the Spirit's functions is to clear up confusion. He dispels darkness and leads us toward light. He purifies us of moral decay and leads us to holiness.

The first time the Spirit appears in the Bible, in the creation account, a beautiful word picture is given. The earth was without form and void, and the Spirit "moved" on the face of the deep. The sense of the Hebrew verb here is of a great bird hovering over the darkness and bringing order out of chaos.[9]

The Holy Spirit works that way inside us as well. If our own understanding is dark, the Spirit brings light. If our understanding is chaotic, the Spirit brings order. In other words, the Spirit is always leading us toward truth.

American Christians seem to be increasingly dependent on human counselors to help them sort out truth. They remind me of the people Paul says are forever seeking the knowledge of truth but never able to come to it.[10] God wants the people who are called by His name to get beyond the childhood stage where they're desperate for the advice of humans. If we seek God and open ourselves to His Word to us, He'll give us His counsel.

Our extreme dependence on human counsel was brought to my attention by James Mbinda, a Ugandan priest, who was visiting my parish. One day he rather bluntly said that he was horrified by the extensive counseling program we have. I responded by defending our ministry, saying how much good it was effecting, how necessary it was. James, however, thought the ideal situation was one where Christians were mature enough to hear God's voice. I still think our counseling ministry is important, but I frequently think about the large element of truth in James's observation. We're too prone to look for some person who will tell us what our next step should be, and not eager enough to listen to and obey the Spirit of truth, who promises to lead us into all truth, but who insists that we walk by faith and not by sight.

Some people claim they don't feel the inner nudgings of the Holy Spirit's counsel, but they probably haven't learned that being willing to follow the counsel or the truth given is a precondition for hearing it. Some people want to know God's will for them only so they can consider it among all the options before them. They tend to make a mental list:

a) What my spouse thinks I should do.
b) What my best friend thinks I should do.
c) What my therapist thinks I should do.
d) What God thinks I should do.

Then they choose, as if it were a cafeteria selection of entrees. Nevertheless, I'm convinced that they won't truly know God's will until after they've settled the question of whether or not they're going to do it.

When someone asks me, "How can I know the will of God?" I respond by saying that he or she is asking the wrong question. The problem is never one of ignorance; believe it or not, the Holy Spirit knows how to get through anyone's thick head! The problem is always one of willingness.

When we're willing to receive and act on the Holy Spirit's counsel, I believe it comes in a "still, small voice." For me, at least, He's never written His will across the sky. Elijah learned that the voice of the Lord wasn't like a strong wind or an earthquake or a roaring fire, but rather a gentle whisper.[11]

A man spoke to me one day who was terribly concerned that he'd never heard God's voice, and it became quickly evident to me that he'd been expecting an audible, measurable sound. Now I won't say that kind of communication is beyond the Spirit's ability; but the Spirit's voice, which I know as surely as I know my wife's voice, is internal. It's so quiet that I can miss it if I don't take the time and effort to shut out the other noises around me and the other noises within myself which tend to demand my attention.

The voice of the Spirit is nearly impossible to describe to someone who isn't a believer. It's like trying to give someone who's blind an understanding of color. If I were to tell someone who'd never had sight that a sunset is streaks of red and yellow against the blue sky, it would all be rather meaningless. I remember hearing of a scientific experiment in which they were trying to explain red to a blind person. This scientist must have been a poet, because he said that red was something like the piercing sound of a trumpet. In one sense that's a perfect analogy, but of course in a literal sense it's totally wrong; sight and sound aren't alike at all.

As in so many other areas of the Christian life, hearing the voice of the Holy Spirit is something we can understand only after we believe. Augustine was right when he said, "I believe in order that I may understand." Like love and marriage, one has to come before the other.

The Ultimate Truth

The ultimate truth to which the Spirit leads us is Jesus, *the* truth. As we said when we looked at the story of Nicodemus, the Spirit implants this truth in our hearts when He takes up residence within us. This is the counsel, the understanding of the kingdom of God, that "the world cannot receive."

First Corinthians 12:3 also speaks of this ultimate truth: "Therefore I want you to understand that no one speaking by the Spirit of God ever says 'Jesus be cursed!' and no one can say 'Jesus is Lord' except by the Holy Spirit." Paul's reference to cursing Jesus is a strong phrase, but we can modify it without changing the truth presented: No one speaking by the Spirit of God ever says or does anything that lowers the Lord Jesus Christ in the estimation of other people. If a person is off-base in reference to who Jesus is, that person is off-base all the way. It's kind of like buttoning a shirt. If you start by putting the wrong button in the wrong hole, the whole line ends up wrong. Jesus is the center around which all truth revolves.

The truth-giving *work* of the Holy Spirit is broader than giving revelation about Jesus, and it's broader than giving personal counsel. There are lesser truths in the universe—scientific truths, literary truths, poetic truths, mathematical truths—and the Spirit of God leads people to truth in all these areas.

Some people try to separate "religious" truth from "secular" truth, but I don't think the world works that way. Two plus two equals four, not six. It always has and it always will—on earth and in heaven. Truth is universal and all truth is God's truth. Let's say a scientist who has no respect for the Lord, who is alienated from Him and does not know Him, discovers a cure for cancer. Any truth that the scientist discovers is God's truth and is revealed to him by the Holy Spirit. Like much of the world, such a scientist is operating on "borrowed capital." They don't realize that the urgency within them leading them on to the truth, prodding them on to the truth, is the Spirit of God. Their abilities and insights come from God even though they don't know Him.

The first line of the book *Metaphysics* by the ancient Greek philosopher Aristotle says, "All men by nature desire knowledge." As there is a thirst in each of us for God, there is a thirst for knowledge and perfection. What made Columbus set sail even though everyone told him he would fall off the edge of the earth? People have sacrificed their lives in order to learn and discover and improve the universe. I believe it's the Holy Spirit who presses everyone on toward perfection, and when we reach it, we recognize it because the Spirit reveals even that to us.

God can and does work through anyone for the improvement of the human race, and we're quite wrong to reject truth just because we don't like its immediate source. The ultimate source is God.

We never need to fear genuine learning. Sadly

enough, however, ever since its earliest years the church has had an anti-intellectual strain running throughout its thought. Tertullian, for example—one of the Latin fathers of the church who lived from 160 to 230—said, ''What has Athens to do with Jerusalem?'' Athens was the symbol of Greek philosophy, and Jerusalem, the symbol of Christian faith. He was obviously implying that all anyone needs is Jerusalem. Yet the Bible doesn't teach all truth on all subjects. Many other items of knowledge are necessary for a well-ordered and balanced life, and we should never be afraid to seek truth, wherever we find it. God doesn't mean for His children to run away from godless teaching, as if hiding our heads in the sand will defend our frail faith. He doesn't want us to climb aboard a rocket and fly off into space in order to escape the world's influence. The Spirit that's within us is greater than the spirit that's in the world;[12] and God intends us to live full-bodied lives *in* the world, because it's the world He came to save, and it's the sphere of our operation.

If we're listening for God's truth, we can't subscribe to a narrowness that puts blinders on our eyes. When the Holy Spirit is within us, our vision is increased and widened, not restricted and bound. But while our vision is being expanded, we're asked to guard the truth within us. Second Timothy 1:13 says, ''Follow the pattern of the sound words which you heard from me, with the faith and love which are in Christ Jesus; guard the truth that has been entrusted to you by the Holy Spirit who dwells within us.''

Just how are we to go about guarding the truth that is residing within our bodies, God's temples? How do we go about appropriating the counsel that is internal, yet not forced upon us? For some answers, let's take a look at what it means to walk in the light—as Jesus Himself is in the light.

Chapter Six

Called to Holiness

When the Holy Spirit takes up residence in us, we're plundered from the house of Satan and brought into the household of faith. We're taken out from under the sovereignty of the evil one and brought under the sovereignty of Jesus Christ.

But when we enter God's kingdom we're not immediately ushered off into heaven so we can dance on the streets paved with gold. Instead, we remain here on the earth where Satan, though ultimately defeated, still likes to go around setting fires, muddying the waters and causing confusion.

I love to set up scenarios of how I would run the world if I were God. If that had been the case, I would have set up a system where Christians were immune to the temptations and wiles of the devil. But God has other plans. He asks that we look to the Spirit and to the Word for our victories and for our direction.

Trials and Temptations

James 1:2 is an amazing verse: "Count it all joy, my brethren, when you meet various trials." The Greek word in this verse translated "trials"—*peirasmoi*—is rendered "temptations" in the King James Version. Perhaps the Phillips paraphrase best shows the term's ambiguous nature by giving both meanings: "When all kinds of *trials and temptations* crowd into your lives, don't resent them as intruders, but welcome them as friends!" (italics mine).

How could James say that trials and temptations can be joyous? He goes on to give a reason: "For you know that the testing of your faith produces steadfastness." This is very hard for some people to understand, but it makes sense when you think of how we humans test the sturdiness of the products we design and manufacture.

Several years ago both Timex and Samsonite televised some great commercials which showed how durable their products were. Suitcases were dropped from airplanes. Watches were taken into the ocean. I've even seen a more recent magazine ad of a certain Bible whose binding is so strong it withstood falling off the roof of a moving car.

Before any company dares to make such claims about its product, it tests and retests the design, the materials and the workmanship. Each time a weakness is found in the construction, they redesign and fortify that spot. In a similar way, God allows our faith to be tested so that we might become Christlike, so that we might become more and more perfect.

A few verses later, James has a further insight into temptation: "Let no one say when he is tempted, 'I am tempted by God'; for God cannot be tempted with evil and he himself tempts no one."[1] Although God *allows* temptation and *uses* it to strengthen His children, He does not Himself entice us. Matthew 4:1 tells what happened to Jesus immediately after His baptism and anointing by the Holy Spirit: "Then Jesus was led up by the Spirit into the wilderness to be tempted by the devil." The Holy Spirit may have wanted Jesus to be strengthened, but the Spirit had nothing to do with the tempting.

Sometimes we view temptation as a test of our will power—which is exactly how Satan would like us to see it, because all of us, in our own strength, would be easy pushovers. But temptations, if seen as God sees them, are tests of faith rather than tests of will.

We must also recognize the difference between a *trial* and a *temptation*. I think trials are often occasions for temptations, occasions when we may turn our vision away from Jesus.

I love to tell the story about a certain day I was riding to a meeting at which I was the speaker. We'd allowed no extra time in our schedule, and—wouldn't you know it—we had a flat tire. Immediately, both the driver and I knew that we'd arrive too late. My friend's first comment was "Look how Satan is hindering us from getting to that meeting." Precisely at the same moment my thought was, *I wonder what God has in mind by allowing this to happen.* If Satan had his way, our trials would be occasions for fretting, complaining, fussing and doubting. But God would have them used for faith building.

The apostle Paul also talks about temptation, and in terms that can and should set us on our way rejoicing: "No temptation has overtaken you that is not common to man. God is faithful, and he will not let you be tempted beyond your strength, but with the temptation will also provide the way of escape."[2]

This verse always makes me think of the story of Job, which starts with a conversation between God and Satan. God almost seems to be boasting a little: "Look at my servant Job, the most righteous man on the earth." Satan said, "Well, what did you expect? After all, everything he ever touched turned to gold; he has a perfect family and everything anyone could ever want. He has no reason to complain. Just let a little trauma come into his life and see how faithful he is."

So the Lord said, "All right. Go ahead and do your worst, but don't touch Job himself."

Satan did his dirty work: In one day Job lost everything—his sheep, his cattle, his camels, his servants and his children. Yet the Scriptures say that Job didn't speak foolishly against God. He didn't take Satan's bait and turn the trials, which in turn were temptations, into sins.

The next scene is back in heaven, where God is again boasting of His servant Job, who remained faithful under attack. Satan, however, wasn't impressed. He knew that our own health is what we value most. So God said, "OK"—and these were His exact words—"He is in your power; only spare his life."[3]

This passage shows who's in control of the temptations that come into a believer's life. God regulates the degree of our trials or temptations.

God is always the supreme commander and He allows Satan to go only so far. We mustn't think of God as being up in heaven wringing His hands over His poor children who are walking along through life being ambushed by the evil one. Satan, we mustn't forget, has been bound.

Attitudes and Actions

A Christian can be tempted and not succumb to sin because of the power of the Holy Spirit. I see the life of a Christian as a journey down a road with a white stripe down the middle. A Christian's desire—the desire of the Spirit within—is to walk down the center of the road, the road of holiness. Although a person doesn't have to be a Christian to have the desire to be good, a person who is not indwelt by the Holy Spirit loves to sin and, from time to time, abandons him or herself to it in such a way that it feels comfortable. When unbelievers sin, they don't experience the agony that comes from walking off the road that is well lit and down into a dark ravine on either side of the road. They're completely adapted to the rough terrain and the darkness, as a fish, totally adapted to its environment, is unaware of the water that surrounds it.

When people become Christians, they find that the attitudes and actions that used to bring them such pleasure are no longer enjoyable; in fact, those same sins produce discomfort and guilt and estrangement from the Comforter within. A man who used to get satisfaction from degrading his wife, for example, gradually finds his actions and words uncomfortably incompatible with the convicting voice of the Spirit.

I'm reminded of a Christian drug and alcohol rehabilitation center called "Pivot House," whose residents worship with our congregation weekly. Occasionally I'll invite one of them to stand and testify to the life-changing power of Christ in his or her life. Admittedly, the changes they report are dramatic, and I can see by the looks on the faces of the congregation whether they are refreshed or repelled by the stories. One night a well-dressed, well-groomed, well-spoken young man stood and told how he'd been a "poly-addict"—one who was hooked on cocaine, heroin and alcohol. He told how he'd been raised in a good home, had gone to Sunday school and had been clean all the way through college. It wasn't until he was a success in his career that he sought "higher" experiences, and in the process he lost his wife, children, career and health. His self-respect was slipping into the gutter as well.

This man knew, however, that one thing was constant—the love and prayers of his mother. He told how that knowledge led him to seek help, and how that love and knowledge of those prayers sustained him through the rehabilitation process, until he had no desire to do anything but serve Jesus. He wanted only to give God the glory and was free of all desire save that of whatever God's will was for him.

In the presence of the congregation he asked for his mother's forgiveness, and his wife's, and his children's. Then he turned to our people and told them that one thing he learned was that we are all sinners, and that some of those listening to him were carrying the burdens of secret sins that were separating them from God as much as his sins had separated him from his family and the path that God had chosen for him to follow.

When it was time to come forward for the receiving of the Eucharist, I saw many tearful faces, including those of clergy. The testimony had touched them deeply. You can't argue with a changed life, and the bigger the change, the stronger the witness. That man has gone through Bible college, been ordained in a Pentecostal denomination and is reunited with his wife. They have a new child, his mother is living with them, and they pastor a small church in Pennsylvania. He regularly helps people over the hurdles they face, not all of which are as dramatic as his own.

At any point on our walk down the road of holy living, we can be tempted to start to wander off and down one of two steep banks. On one side, let's say the left, we can veer off if we go ahead and do something we know God doesn't want us to do. When we get close to the edge, we can sense that our inner lights are flashing and bells are ringing; that's the voice of the Holy Spirit trying to get us back to the center of the road. If, when we hear the warning, we yield the matter to the Lord, He'll disincline us from yielding to the sin and center us back on the path.

The ditch on the other side of the road, the right side, is equally dangerous and dark. We can walk over that edge when we don't do something we believe God wants us to do. When we get too close to that edge the lights start flashing again and the bells go off, indicating that we're not yielding to the Lord. The Spirit of God within, the law written on our hearts, inclines us toward or gives us the desire to stay in the center of the road—not because we have to but because we want to.

First John 3:9 talks about this walk in holiness: "No one born of God commits sin; for God's nature abides in him, and he cannot sin because he is born of God." And that's not all; John keeps going: "By this it may be seen who are the children of God, and who are the children of the devil: whoever does not do right is not of God, nor he who does not love his brother."

Can John really mean what he's saying? At various times in Christian history, theologians have taken these several verses and said, "Well, if you're born again, you cannot sin; you never yield to temptation." They've taught that Christians can and should lead lives of sinless perfection. But this viewpoint has prompted people to be dishonest with themselves and with God. In fact, in the same book of 1 John, which was written to Christians, the apostle says, "If we say we have no sin, we deceive ourselves, and the truth is not in us."[4]

So what can it mean—"No one born of God commits sin"? The key is found in the Greek grammar of the passage, which is not apparent in the English. The verb tense is progressive, relaying the idea that the believer does not *habitually continue* to walk in sin. All of us have lapses from time to time; all of us have failures. But the person who is born of the Spirit does not make a habit of sinning. The Spirit of God within us never produces anything sinful, so as we learn to listen to and obey the Spirit, we gradually walk more and more in harmony with the will of God.

The apostle Paul knew that, despite the law written in his heart, despite nudgings of the Spirit within, he sometimes felt a struggle. To the church at Rome he wrote, "I find it to be a law that when I want to do right, evil lies close at hand. I delight in the law of God in my inmost self, but I see in my members another law at war with the law of my mind and making me captive to the law of sin which dwells in my members."[5]

At this point in Paul's life, he was in the throes of a strong internal conflict. In fact, he felt utterly defeated. We Christians are often in a similar situation. We fall and do what we know the Spirit doesn't want us to do, then we panic and think the Holy Spirit has left us. This is especially true of new Christians who, when they're first converted, seem to experience heaven on earth.

Everything they see reflects the glory of God; they're filled with praise from the moment they get up until the moment they go to sleep. They find themselves saying, or at least thinking, "I'm never again going to do an evil thing." But then, after awhile, the sin that's in them begins to reassert itself. Satan hits them in their weak spot and they don't rely on the Spirit for His strength. What they, and we, must realize, is that sin in a believer's life can obscure the light of the Spirit's presence, the warmth of His love and the assurance of His counsel—but it does *not* send Him running!

I happened to be in Vancouver, Canada, on a day when the moon totally eclipsed the sun. At 10 a.m. my world went dark and cold. If I hadn't known that the moon had come between the sun and the earth, I might have thought that the sun had gone away. But it hadn't, just as the Holy Spirit doesn't leave His children. Whether we feel or believe it, the Holy Spirit is within us. He is there, still within us despite our sin, because our salvation is not dependent on our righteousness— but on our appropriation of Jesus' righteousness. So even though we're called to resist temptation, to walk in the light of the Spirit, to guard the truth that's within us, our holiness is never the means of our salvation.

Paul knew this even in the midst of his temporary defeat, which he continued to describe to the Romans by asking, "Wretched man that I am! Who will deliver me from this body of death?" Yet the answer was immediately on his lips, for he added, "Thanks be to God through Jesus Christ our Lord!"

If Paul hadn't gone on to write chapter 8 of Romans, we might conclude that Paul was describing the entire Christian experience as one defeat after another. But

Paul continues by saying, "There is therefore now no condemnation for those who are in Christ Jesus."[6]

We must recognize the great difference between *conviction* and *condemnation*. In John 16:9 Jesus told His disciples that the Holy Spirit would "convict the world of sin," and His convicting work is as much a part of the lives of believers as unbelievers. Nevertheless, in the life of a Christian, conviction does not include a condemning and overwhelming guilt that settles in like heavy fog. At times we may hear a condemning question whose inflection relays a sense of horror: "How could *you*, a *Christian*, *do* something like that?" But we can be sure that kind of accusation comes from Satan, not the Holy Spirit. The Spirit shines light on our sin for the sole purpose of guiding us back to the center of the road or back into perfect fellowship with our Holy God.

Conviction to Confession

Whenever we feel this correcting, counseling conviction, we're asked to confess our sin. The book of 1 John—again, written to Christians—says: "If we confess our sins, he is faithful and just, and will forgive our sins and cleanse us from all unrighteousness....My little children, I am writing this to you so that you may not sin; but if any one does sin, we have an advocate with the Father, Jesus Christ the righteous."[7]

What does the word "confess" mean? It involves agreeing with the convicting Spirit—saying, "Yes, you're right. I was wrong, and I'm sorry"—then turning back toward the truth and asking forgiveness.

The German theologian Dietrich Bonhoeffer was once asked, "To whom should we confess?" He replied that we should confess to "one who lives beneath the cross."

Bonhoeffer would not recommend confessing to someone who was only a psychiatrist or a psychologist, trained in the knowledge of human weaknesses, but not trained in the knowledge of God. If we know only the spirit and nature of humanity, but not our sin nature and the freeing power of the Holy Spirit, then cleansing does not come.

God's kind of forgiveness is foreign to our human way of thinking. Sadly enough, we tend to "forgive but not forget"—not only the sins of others, but also our own sins. But the Scriptures refer to God's forgiveness in three different ways: He takes our sins and casts them behind His back[8]; in other words, He puts our sins out of His sight. He separates our sins from us as far as the east is from the west[9]; in other words, He puts our sins out of His reach. Finally, when He forgives our sins, He remembers them against us no more[10]; He puts our sins out of His mind.

Over a period of time, as we listen to and obey the convicting counsel of the Spirit, our spiritual defeats can decrease in number and frequency. Later on in Romans 8, Paul says: "For those who live according to the flesh set their minds on the things of the flesh, but those who live according to the Spirit set their minds on the things of the Spirit."[11] To the Galatians Paul again speaks of a Christian's journey: "Walk by the Spirit, and do not gratify the desires of the flesh. For the desires of the flesh are against the Spirit, and the desires of the Spirit are against the flesh; for these are opposed to each other, to prevent you from doing what you would. But if you are led by the Spirit you are not under the law."[12]

Here Paul is reminding Christians that their old sinful

nature wars against the Spirit of holiness and truth that's within them. He refers here to his flesh as if it were a force contrary to the Holy Spirit. Since the word "flesh" has several different meanings in Greek and in English, Paul's usage can easily be misunderstood. Sometimes the word "flesh" refers to our bodies—our physical as opposed to our spiritual nature. We mortals are fleshly beings, while the angels apparently are not. When the word is used in that way, it's describing something that shouldn't be put down.

Throughout history many Christians have considered the body evil. But that train of thought can be traced back to the Greek philosophy of Plato—who had very distinct definitions of body, soul and spirit—rather than to the New Testament, which instead presents the body as the "neutral" house of the Spirit. A biblical view of the human body insists that it can be used for good or for evil. In another usage, the word *flesh* refers to the whole world order opposed to God. In this sense our sins are fleshly—whether or not they're bodily. The second definition is the one used here by Paul.

Works of the Flesh

I'm convinced that the hot breath of God will ultimately destroy all our works that aren't of the Spirit. Isaiah 40:6-7 paints a startling picture of this reality: "All flesh is as grass....The grass withers, the flower fades, when the breath of the Lord blows upon it." You and I are accustomed to thinking of the Holy Spirit as breathing *life*. We believe in the Holy Spirit, the giver of life, who fashioned and then breathed into Adam, who gives new life to those who are called by His name; but here is a case where the Spirit was breathing death on something. But on what was He breathing death? On

all that was and is of the flesh. The more open we are
to the Holy Spirit, the more we find actions and attitudes
dying in us; and they're dying under His influence at
the same time other actions and attitudes are being made
alive.

Galatians 5 goes on to list the works of the flesh, the
sins that the Spirit within us abhors: "Now the works
of the flesh are plain: immorality, impurity, licentiousness, idolatry, sorcery, enmity, strife, jealousy, anger,
selfishness, dissension, party spirit, envy, drunkenness,
carousing, and the like."[13] Let's look at a few of these
desires Paul tells us not to gratify.

Immorality, or fornication, is sexual relationships outside of marriage. I once saw a hotel sign that said,
"Have your next affair with us." I've chosen to believe
they were advertising their banquet facilities, but I'm
sure the sign was intentionally ambiguous and sugges-
tive. That's the kind of culture we live in. Illicit sex
might bring momentary pleasure, of course, but it can't
produce happiness. Of course sex is perfectly natural
and it's fun—but it was meant to function only within
the context of commitment between one man and one
woman. When it's taken out of that context, it all goes
awry. Unfortunately, the sin of fornication compounds
itself, as babies conceived out of wedlock are aborted
by the millions. Sexual liberation is, in fact, not liberation at all, but rather bondage—a bondage in which God
has no part.

Impurity is also a sexual sin, but more broadly defined. I would put pornography in this category. Licentiousness is sexuality gone wild, so that it dominates
every conscious moment. Are you aware that there are
twice as many pornographic bookstores in America as

there are McDonald's restaurants? I'm encouraged that many Christians are working to get this material out of the public eye, but let's not fool ourselves. Pornography may no longer be sold in the local drug store, but it's still being produced, and unfortunately it's still being secretly bought and read under the cover of darkness by Christians who rationalize that their lust isn't adultery, as Jesus said it was. Licentiousness is a more common problem than we think.

Idolatry is a sin many Christians relegate to India, Africa and Asia, where some people worship graven idols. But let me give you a definition of God that a professor once gave me. He said that a person's god was his or her ultimate concern. Some people make their careers their gods; they'd sacrifice their families, their integrity, their health for their titles—or for their bosses' titles. Some people make their family into their god. Don't get me wrong, our families are important to us, but the Lord makes it clear that He is to be our ultimate concern—over and above any human. Any other ultimate concern is an idol.

Sorcery involves clairvoyance, including horoscopes, which millions of sophisticated, educated Americans read and live by. Many more say, "Oh, I just glance at it for fun," which is like a child saying that he plays with matches for fun.

Enmity, strife, dissension and party spirit are all essentially synonymous. They are works of the flesh that divide people from each other and cause a "we" versus "they" syndrome, which is never the work of the Holy Spirit.

We should remember that the list actually goes on and on. Paul doesn't, and couldn't, enumerate all our sins here. He simply ends by saying, "and the like," just as the king of Siam always said, "et cetera, et cetera, et cetera," in "The King and I." All works of the flesh—whether listed here or not—are not of God, and they will not be blessed. On the contrary, they'll be destroyed, as heat destroys dry grass.

Fruit of the Spirit

Paul doesn't just tell us what actions and attitudes to turn from. He goes on to list as well the fruit of the Spirit, godly qualities that grow within us as a result of the Holy Spirit's residence there: "But the fruit of the Spirit is love, joy, peace, patience, kindness, goodness, faithfulness, gentleness, self-control."[14]

Learning to walk by—or in—the Spirit doesn't happen overnight. All fruit takes time to mature and ripen. The fruit of the Spirit is just that—produced by the Spirit's work in us, not by our own efforts. The fruit won't grow if we don't water it by yielding to the Spirit's counsel, to the law written on our hearts; but we, in our own strength, don't bring forth the growth.

One thing is sure: God is out to perfect us, and He's given us everything we need—guidance, direction, nurture, truth, conviction—to walk in His ways and live for His glory.

Part Four

The Spirit Upon You

Chapter Seven

Pentecostal Power

I know you're wondering how I could get more than half way through a book on the Holy Spirit without mentioning Pentecost, the feast day that's often celebrated as the anniversary of the coming of the Holy Spirit. You can be sure I haven't said all there is to say about the work of the Spirit without considering what happened fifty days after Jesus' resurrection.

The last chapter of Luke takes place before Jesus' ascension and after He had summarized the Old Testament prophesies about Himself—that He would die, that He would rise on the third day, and that repentance and forgiveness of sins would be preached in His name. In that chapter Jesus said, "And behold, I send the promise of my Father to you; but stay in the city, until you are clothed with power from on high."[1]

The phrase "the promise of my Father" doesn't occur anywhere else in the four Gospels. Whatever it is, it seems to have something to do with power, and the disciples needed it. Luke repeated these mysterious last words of Jesus in the first chapter of the Acts of the Apostles, but there Jesus is quoted as giving a little more explanation of what they're to wait for: "John baptized with water, but before many days you shall be baptized with the Holy Spirit."[2]

Jesus seems to have been saying, "You know who I am, what I am. In these last forty days since my resurrection, I've carefully instructed you about God's kingdom—My role and your roles in it. You've received the Holy Spirit. Yet there is one thing you lack: the promise of the Father, the baptism in the Holy Spirit."

Then Jesus continued to explain what the disciples lacked: "You shall receive power when the Holy Spirit has come upon you; and you shall be my witnesses in Jerusalem, and in all Judea, and Samaria, and to the ends of the earth."[3] Jerusalem was the city in which all this took place. Judea was the province which included Jerusalem. Samaria was the province just to the north. "The ends of the earth" are obvious. The disciples needed power to carry out the mission God had given them, which was to spread the news of His redemption to the entire world.

God's way of working boggles my mind. What a seemingly clumsy arrangement—making the salvation of mankind dependent upon the slender thread of human preaching. If I'd wanted to get that news out, I would have endowed angels, perhaps archangels, so eloquent and awesome that no one would resist their message. But God chose and still chooses to accomplish His purposes through mortals who have received His power.

In some respects, the baptism of the Holy Spirit is

like the Old Testament anointing: The Spirit comes *upon* a person, empowering him or her for ministry. But the word "baptize" is a much stronger word than "anointing". In Greek, "baptize" is what you might call a "secular" rather than a "religious" word. When a piece of unbleached muslin was plunged into a huge vat of bright red dye, it was baptized—saturated, covered over, put under—so that it totally took on the new color. Not one corner would be left untouched and uncovered. Jesus deliberately used this vivid word to indicate His desire for God's children to be completely saturated with the Holy Spirit. He wants the Spirit, who is within us, also to be upon us, to cover us, to saturate us, so that we take upon ourselves the character of the Holy Spirit.

Waiting for the Wind

After Jesus had ascended to His Father, I can just imagine impetuous Peter getting impatient and saying, "Why should we wait? Let's go out and tell everyone we meet what we know about the Lord. Let's get on with it!"

And I can hear some of the other ten disciples saying, "But, Peter, He told us to wait...."

Luke tells us that a total of 120 people did wait, and that ten days after Jesus' ascension, the Wind swept through the group, prompting them to leave the building they had been in and to hit the streets preaching the good news. Peter, who seven weeks before hadn't had the power to admit that he was a follower of Jesus, now preached quite a sermon to a most skeptical crowd:

"Jesus of Nazareth, a man attested to you by God with mighty works and wonders and signs which God did through him in your midst—this Jesus, delivered up according to the definite plan and foreknowledge of

God, you, crucified and killed....This Jesus God raised up, and of that we all are witnesses....Let all the
house of Israel know assuredly that God has made him
both Lord and Christ, this Jesus whom you
crucified."[4]

At the end of the sermon, Luke reports, those who
were listening were "cut to the heart," and they asked
Peter how they should respond. (I think Paul calls the
Word of God the sword of the Spirit[5] because it cuts
like a surgeon's scalpel—in order to heal.) Peter
answered that the people should "repent, and be baptized...in the name of Jesus Christ for the forgiveness
of your sins; and you shall receive the gift of the Holy
Spirit. For the promise is to you and to your children
and to all that are far off, every one whom the Lord
our God calls to him."

Luke then says that three thousand people became
Christians that day. Peter's witness, his preaching forth
of the Word, was powerful because of the anointing of
the Holy Spirit upon him.

Power With a Purpose

This two-part work of the Holy Spirit—His coming
within and upon a person—is also evident in the life of
the apostle Paul. If you were to say that Paul—or Saul,
as he was known then—was converted on the road to
Damascus, you'd be right. The Lord appeared to him
and stopped him in his tracks. Right then, Paul
acknowledged Jesus as Lord and became a Christian.
Yet something happened to him three days later, when
an obscure disciple by the name of Ananias laid hands
on Paul: The Spirit of God came upon him and he began
the missionary ministry to which he was called.[6]

On Pentecost the baptism of the Spirit was accompanied by dramatic signs—the roar of wind, tongues of fire upon people's heads, the disciples' speaking forth in tongues. When Paul received the baptism, his sight, which had been lost upon his conversion, was restored. But just as every conversion is not as dramatic as Paul's, not every baptism of the Spirit is accompanied by immediate signs and wonders.

The Lord wants to give us His power, and He does give His power, even if no signs or feelings are experienced. The purpose of the baptism of the Holy Spirit is not to give a warm, slushy feeling deep down inside. That may accompany the baptism, but its purpose is to empower us to do God's work.

How do we receive this baptism? By yielding and by asking. Remember the story of Jesus' standing at the temple on the feast day, watching the gigantic water jars being poured across the pavement. Standing there, he said, "If anyone thirst, let him come to me and drink. He who believes in me, as the Scripture says, out of his heart shall flow rivers of living water."

John, the apostle who wrote this story down after Jesus' resurrection and ascension, went on to add an explanation of Jesus' words: "Now this he said about the Spirit, whom those who believed in him were to receive; for as yet the Spirit had not been given, because Jesus was not yet glorified." Jesus was glorified when He ascended to the Father. The power of the Spirit was then released upon the disciples and, in turn, upon any believer who is willing to yield his or her life to God's purpose.

I often say that some Christians are more effective in their service than others, not because they have any more of the Holy Spirit than their brothers or sisters, but because the Holy Spirit has more of them. The yieldedness that releases God's power upon them opens the channel through which the Holy Spirit can flow out of them like the "rivers of living water" John described. First Corinthians 12:13 says that all Christians have been "made to drink of one Spirit," but God also intends that Christians should overflow with evidence that the Spirit within them is a holy and powerful one, that they commune with the Holy Spirit so closely and constantly that their ministries become all God would have them be.

Chapter Eight

Called to a Mission

Just as God had a task for each of the apostles, He wants each of His children to bring blessing to other believers, to bring glory to His name, and to be channels that bring His light and truth to the unbelieving world. Three of the four gospels—Matthew, Mark and Luke—report Jesus' last words as commands to the disciples, and in turn to us, to spread the good news of salvation across the lands. Matthew 28:18 adds an interesting phrase to this commission: "All authority in heaven and on earth has been given to me. Go therefore...." Jesus' possession of all authority makes it not only possible but necessary for us to take the message of the gospel to the whole earth. We can and should "move out" to make disciples on the basis of His authority. God hasn't called us all to be preaching evangelists like Peter or itinerant missionaries like Paul. But Ephesians 2:10 says that we're all "His workmanship, created for Christ Jesus for good works which God prepared beforehand that we should walk in them.''

The good works—the ministry—that God sets before each of us are not brownie points we chalk up so we'll be acceptable to God. None of us will stand before God and be able to appeal for His mercy on the basis of our church committee work, our twenty years of Sunday school teaching, or our generous, even sacrificial, church offerings.

Other religions are based on salvation by works— the belief that we can, by actions and behavior, make ourselves acceptable before God. Buddhists climb up the Eight-fold Path; they mustn't stop at the second rung of the ladder. Moslems observe five rituals: reciting of a creed, "There is no god but Allah, and Muhammad is his Prophet"; praying five times a day facing the east; giving alms to the poor; fasting during the month of Ramadan; and making a once-in-a-lifetime pilgrimage to Mecca. Why? To make themselves acceptable to Allah. But all their attempts—and all our attempts—to earn God's favor are as futile as were Adam and Eve's pitiable fig-leaf aprons, which didn't cover their nakedness from God's sight.

Isaiah 64:6 states that our righteousness—not our sins, mind you, but our righteousness—is filthy rags to our holy God.[1] We don't work our way into the favor of God. As Christians, we're accepted by Him on the basis of grace through faith in Jesus Christ.

Although the works God has planned for us don't initiate God's grace, they are by-products of a vibrant faith, just as our holiness is. James the brother of Jesus said that anyone who claims to have faith but has no accompanying works doesn't have the kind of faith that justifies in the sight of God.[2] A man who boasts that because he's been saved he can "live like the devil" has no understanding of the nature of salvation, for we were created for good works which were "prepared beforehand."

Planned for Power

The phrase has been used so much that it's a cliche, but yes, God does have a "plan for your life." In an Old Testament conversation with Jeremiah, God makes it clear that He prepares a person's good works ahead of his or her time. Jeremiah wrote, "Now the word of the Lord came to me saying, Before I formed you in the womb I knew you, and before you were born I consecrated you; I appointed you a prophet to the nations.' "

But Jeremiah's immediate response was fear. He said, "Ah, Lord God! Behold, I do not know how to speak, for I am only a youth."[3] Nevertheless, despite this initial reaction, Jeremiah accepted God's call to good works, for the next fifty chapters of his book are full of the prophecies the Lord spoke through Jeremiah's lips. The New Testament as well shows how the Holy Spirit has specific plans for the spreading of the gospel. Acts 13:2,4-5 says, "While they were worshiping the Lord and fasting, the Holy Spirit said, 'Set apart for me Barnabas and Saul for the work to which I have called them.'...So, being sent out by the Holy Spirit, they went down to Seleucia; and from there they sailed to Cyprus. When they arrived at Salamis, they proclaimed the word of God in the synagogues of the Jews...."

Just as God has plans for individual lives, He has plans for the church as a whole. I like to call the Holy Spirit the "executor of the church"—the One who calls the shots, the Central Intelligence. And He can lead groups of people to a consensus concerning His plans—if they're listening.

The vestry of our parish operates under this principle of consensus. I've often told the story of a particular member of our vestry who was the lone dissenting vote on a particular issue. He was absolutely certain that he had heard the voice of the Lord and that the rest of the vestry had not. Meeting after meeting passed, and no action was taken on the matter because of the lack of consensus. Finally, one week another vestry member announced that he now agreed with the dissenter. Then another said the same, and another, until it came to light that the entire vestry had changed its mind! Not one word was spoken outside of the meeting about the issue. The Lord had simply changed their hearts. Had that one man acquiesced, the item of business might have been acted upon in a way that didn't reflect the will of the Lord for the parish. We would have forfeited the blessings of obedience if we hadn't waited for a consensus.

Sadly enough, though God is willing to make His plans known, at any stage of our call to ministry our free will can block the channel through which we receive His empowerment, and through which the "rivers of living water" flow out of us. Once again, I know what I would have done if I were God. I would not have created a species capable of defying me. I would have decided to make each person like a computer; I would stick a card in each back so that every individual would march through life fulfilling all the good works I had prepared for him or her to walk in. Each card would be perfectly programmed for a specific individual, and nothing could ever happen that didn't fit into the plan. Or, if I'd wanted to think in more traditionally artistic terms, I would have created people as puppets. When I pulled one string, the puppet would do a good work. When I pulled another string, the deed would vary. And I, being God, would never pull a wrong string.

Nevertheless, God created us with wills of our own. Even after we've become His children, even after His Spirit is residing within us, we can still choose to live outside the plan of good works He's prepared for us.

One incident in the life of Moses illustrates how our lack of faith can keep us from grabbing hold of the work set before us. The third chapter of Exodus tells the story of God speaking to Moses through a burning bush. This was no "Good morning, how are you?" chat; God had a mission for Moses to complete. In verse 10, the Lord says, "Come, I will send you to Pharaoh that you may bring forth my people, the sons of Israel, out of Egypt."

God was calling Moses to confront the pharaoh and ask for the release of a whole nation of slaves who were working for him—maybe building his pyramid. This conversation between God and Moses was quite lengthy and included miraculous signs of God's power. But before it was finished the enormity of the task to which Moses was being called started to sink in. Moses finally exclaimed, "Oh, my Lord, I am not eloquent...but I am slow of speech and of tongue."

What was Moses doing? He was turning inward and seeing all the reasons why he couldn't accomplish the mission God had planned for him. Such an "I can't talk" excuse is only one of hundreds that we're capable of manufacturing. Most of them are based on our lacks, but one of the best I've ever come across was a righteous-sounding "I'm not worthy to do this task." Several years ago I asked one of our lay leaders if he would consider becoming the senior warden of the parish. He thought that would be quite impossible, as he wasn't worthy of the position. I heartily agreed with him: "You certainly are not. But now that we've come to an agreement on that point, will you be the warden?"

Since none of us is worthy of being in the service of our King, that excuse should be dismissed immediately. Yet it's still used (with many others as well) until such excuses become the spiritual cholesterol that clogs the vessels through which the Spirit wishes to flow, to accomplish His purposes through our planned good works.

But how can we know what good works God is calling us to? God may have spoken to Moses through a burning bush, but—as I said in the last chapter—the Holy Spirit talks to me in whispers to which I must be attuned.

The most powerful radio station in Brazil can be received across the entire country, which is about the size of the continental United States. The station is owned by the Pentecostal Church and is geared to a culture much different from our own. The station's broadcast pattern is unique: Every ten minutes allows for five minutes of music, two minutes of reading a Scripture verse, and a total of three minutes of checking the time at ten-second intervals in between. This round-the-clock pattern is interrupted twice a day—once in the morning and once in the afternoon—with the broadcast of the musical note "A," which is sustained for what seems like forever but is probably only a minute or two. This unusual signal is a service to the musicians across the country. Even those who are in the upper regions of the Amazon can tune in and adjust their instruments. When I visited Brazil and heard of this practice, I immediately saw the similarity between the needs of the musicians and our needs as Christians. We both need to tune in and tune up twice a day!

Just as the radio station sends forth the signal that allows the musicians to stay in tune, so God sends us His direction in the form of His counsel and His power. The question is never, Will God show me or speak to me? The question is whether or not we're prepared to receive the transmission. Do we have the "radio" plugged in, the power turned on and the dial set to the right frequency?

By Nature and by Grace

God equips people for a life of good works in two different but equally important ways: by nature and by grace. When college students ask my advice about sorting out God's plan for their careers, I always turn the question around and ask them what they *like* to do. Too often they look at me in amazement; they were expecting some complicated theological answer and not an invitation to start the decision-making process by looking at who they are. They think of the will of God as something at the end of a treasure hunt, something disconnected from who they, by nature, are. So I ask this question to help a young person identify his or her natural talents (most people enjoy what they're good at), which are God-given for one purpose—to use for His glory.

I don't believe the Holy Spirit makes a practice of leading us down paths that seem to be heading in a direction opposing our natural aptitudes. With absolute certainty I can say that I will never be the president of the Chase Manhattan Bank. It didn't require any revelation from heaven for me to realize that I have no mind for numbers. Just the thought of balancing a checkbook fills me with horror. Even with a calculator, the columns never equal each other—so in our house my wife, the banker, handles the money and gives me my weekly allowance.

I love the story of the farmer who was plowing a field when he happened to look up into the sky and see the clouds arranged in two large letters: P.C. Without a doubt, he knew it was a message for him: that he was to preach Christ. He left the farm, went to school and took a church—which died under his leadership. He went to a second church and that congregation also shriveled up. One day he was explaining his pastoral call to a woman who seemed wise in the ways of the Lord. When he described the message of the clouds— preach Christ—the woman quickly contradicted him. "Oh no," she said, "that's not what it meant at all. The letters stood for plant corn." Now preaching Christ may seem like a much holier vocation than planting corn, but 1 Corinthians 12:5 says, "There are varieties of service, but the same Lord." I was raised in a sub-culture that said a person who wanted to serve the Lord had two options: being a minister or a missionary. Until quite recently, devout Roman Catholics seemed to have only one option. Depending on their sex, they could become a priest or a nun. But the call of God is to a life of service, which can be packaged in a variety of shapes—physician, homemaker, plumber, checkbook-balancer—depending on a person's natural endowments.

Surveys seem to indicate that well over 80 percent of America's work force doesn't find fulfillment in its employment. I think that says something about our spiritual condition as well. Why? Because a person who is listening to the Spirit will be led into an area that will nourish his or her talents and creativity until they blossom. "For I know the plans I have for you, says the Lord, plans for welfare and not for evil, to give you a future and a hope."[4]

In this discussion of the natural way God equips us for ministry, I'd like to step beyond saying we should take our talents into consideration when looking for the good works God has planned for us. We're also called to be good stewards of the resources put—by God—at our disposal. We're *responsible* for what He has placed in our care.

In Matthew 25 Jesus tells a story which has come to be called the parable of the talents.[5] In Greek, the word "talent" actually refers to a measure of weight; you might have had five talents of gold hidden in the back yard, or you might have had ten talents of grain for sale. But I don't think we do violence to this parable if we use the word "talents" as we commonly do today—to refer to God-given abilities. (In fact, our modern word "talent" actually came into the English language through this biblical parable.) Jesus' story is rather simple. A wealthy man preparing to go on a journey calls all his servants together and entrusts his assets to them. He retains ownership but "contracts out" the management of his possessions. He gives five talents to one man, two to another, and one to the third—"each according to his ability."

While the rich man is gone, the servant who has been given the care of the five talents invests them, eventually doubling his money. The man given two talents does equally well, doubling the value of the original money in the same amount of time. The one given the single talent hides the measure of money in the ground—maybe so no one will steal it.

When the master comes back to town, he calls them all in to settle up the accounts. He praises the two who invested and multiplied his money. To both of them he gives the same commendation, "Well done, good and faithful servant; you have been faithful over a little, I will set you over much; enter into the joy of your master." But the lord has harsh words for the man who buried the one talent in his care. Here's their conversation: First, the servant explains, "Master, I knew you to be a hard man, reaping where you did not sow, and gathering where you did not winnow; so I was afraid, and I went and hid your talent in the ground. Here you have what is yours."

But the master answered him, "You wicked and slothful servant! You knew that I reap where I have not sowed, and gather where I have not winnowed? Then you ought to have invested my money with the bankers, and at my coming I should have received what was my own with interest."

What a contrast in responses: a praising "good and faithful servant" as opposed to a condemning "you wicked and slothful servant." The man who buried his talent in the ground said that he did so out of healthy, cautious fear. But the master viewed things differently. He called the man lazy, even wicked, for not even putting the talent in a passbook savings account.

Although we're called to "invest" responsibly our own God-given, natural talents, I don't think we have to go around looking for talents we don't have. What

God holds us accountable for is in direct proportion to what He gives us. The man who doubled his two talents was commended just as highly as the man who doubled the five. The master revealed no "hidden agenda" that upon his return he expected everyone to present him with ten talents.

I'm astounded at the number of people who tell me there's nothing they can do for God. They think this way only because they compare themselves with someone else whom they admire who has obviously been given five talents to start with. Strictly speaking, what any of us can't do is totally irrelevant. If you truly can't do something—and only you know whether the root of your "I can't" is laziness, fear or lack of talent—then you can be sure that God doesn't intend for you to minister in that form. You can rest in your efforts to concentrate on being a good steward of the talent, even if it is singular, that you have been given.

Only for His Purposes

Most of what I've said so far about our natural talents and the part they play in our being equipped for the service to which we've been called could have been part of a workshop given in a secular corporation. It doesn't sound much different from what you might hear from the human potential movement, which places a great emphasis on helping people develop their abilities.

For Christians, however, this natural equipping is only half the story. We're also equipped for service by God's grace—by the empowering or anointing of the Holy Spirit—as were the disciples at Pentecost.

You can be sure that God doesn't plan anyone's life of service and then expect that person to blunder along doing the best he or she can. The Christian faith is not meant to be a do-it-yourself operation. God wants to empower us, and He does so as we yield our wills to His, as we put our talents at His disposal. If we are listening to and willing to obey the voice of God, He empowers us for service. At the same time, however, He never empowers us to fulfill our own purposes or to accomplish our own plans. His power is available only for His purpose: enlarging His kingdom.

Acts 8 tells an interesting story of a man offering the apostles money, thinking he could buy their power—the power of the Holy Spirit—so that he could, in turn, dispense it. He said, "Peter, give me also this power, that any one on whom I lay my hands may receive the Holy Spirit."

Peter's response was harsh. The Revised Standard Version says, "Your silver perish with you, because you thought you could obtain the gift of God [the Spirit of God] with money!" The original Greek words are much more graphic, though not one bit out of place in this situation. A literal translation would be: "To hell with you and your money." Peter wanted quickly to get things straight: The power of the Spirit was and is free to take as we would a gift; it's available to anyone—but never to fulfill personal purposes.

I believe every person alive, no matter how godless a reprobate he or she might be, would like to have the full power of God in his or her life. But many people, like this man whose name was Simon, would like the assistance of God to do their own thing. They want a genie they can command. They want to control God and be the dispenser of His power and blessings—to be able to tell someone, "Yes, be empowered by the Holy Spirit," and then tell someone else, "No, I'm sorry.

The power isn't available to you, but I'll pray for you."
But that's never the way God works. The only way to
experience God's power in our ministries is to find the
purpose for our ministries, and then pursue that purpose—in faith.

The natural talents God gives and His supernatural
empowerment work together, not against each other.
I like to think that our talents show us whether we should
start walking north, south, east, or west, and then the
Holy Spirit gives us the added strength we need to run
instead of plod along on the path that's before us.

Another Moses story shows how the powerful work
of the Holy Spirit heightens a person's natural abilities.
When God told Moses to construct a tabernacle in which
He would reside, He gave very specific building plans.
Moses, a God-gifted leader, was not a gifted craftsman,
and God had someone else in mind to be contractor.
In Exodus 31:1, when Moses is still up on Mount Sinai,
the Lord says to him, "See, I have called by name
Bezalel . . . and I have filled him with the Spirit of God
with ability and intelligence, with knowledge and all
craftsmanship, to devise artistic designs, to work in gold,
silver, and bronze, in cutting stones for setting, and in
carving wood, for work in every craft."

I once heard someone interpret this passage to say
that the Spirit came upon a common, ordinary, unskilled
man and transformed him into an exceptionally talented
artisan. But I don't believe that view for a moment.
Why? Because the Holy Spirit works in us, not to give
us abilities we never before had, but to heighten the
talents we've always had.

I've never known anyone or even heard of anyone
who, under the anointing of the Holy Spirit, was given

a talent that he or she didn't previously possess. I have, however, known of people who've been so freed by the power of the Holy Spirit upon them that they've discovered abilities they didn't know they had.

Think back again to Moses at the burning bush. I believe Moses might have had a God-given talent for public speaking. It may have been hidden even from him, but if he'd sought God's purposes with his whole heart, the talent would have been released by the power of God. God would have empowered Moses to speak directly to the pharaoh if Moses had, by faith, accepted that empowerment.

How can we Christians most effectively carry out God's plan for us? What the church needs is not more expansive facilities, flashy programs or better-trained preachers. God's work can't be done by human effort alone, no matter how many talents He passes around or how intent we are on investing them and multiplying them. What the church needs—what individual Christians need—is more of the releasing, freeing, heightening power of the Holy Spirit that comes with our saying yes to His will. Only we can limit the power of God in our lives and in our churches.

Chapter Nine

The Evidence of the Spirit

We've seen that the Holy Spirit empowers us to perform good works by using and heightening the irrevocable talents He placed within us before we were born. In addition to that empowering, He desires to show forth His presence in temporary spurts to accomplish specific tasks or meet specific needs within the body of Christ.

We must always keep in mind that the Spirit is like the wind—invisible. Christina Rossetti wrote a great little poem about the wind that reminds us of its nature:

Who has seen the wind? Neither you nor I;
But when the trees bow down their heads
The wind is passing by.

That's exactly the way it is when the Holy Spirit manifests Himself, or makes Himself evident, through us. We never see the Spirit; we see only what He accomplishes. Despite His invisibility, however, He intends to operate through individuals in visible ways. Because of the spiritual nature of His being, the Wind makes His hidden presence known by "rustling" us, His leaves.

We can illustrate in yet another way how the manifestations of the Spirit work, although this example makes me very uncomfortable: It shows the negative aspect of a principle which, in the case of the Holy Spirit, is positive.

Let's say you become sick and feel bad enough, for long enough, that you go to the doctor, who says, "What's the trouble?" After you describe how you feel, the doctor looks you over and sees red blotches on your skin. The thermometer indicates that your temperature is above normal. Your throat is irritated. Because the doctor has been carefully trained to "read" outward symptoms, he or she can make conclusions about the disease that's within you. But the physician sees the manifestation of the disease, not the disease itself.

The same principle is at work on a spiritual level. The Holy Spirit makes His presence known by manifesting Himself in ways frequently called "the gifts of the Spirit." In 1 Corinthians 12:8-11, Paul presents the most complete (though not exhaustive) list and explanation of these gifts:

"To one is given through the Spirit the utterance of wisdom, and to another the utterance of knowledge according to the same Spirit, to another faith by the same Spirit, to another gifts of healing by the one Spirit, to another the working of miracles, to another prophecy, to another the ability to distingush between spirits, to another various kinds of tongues. All these are inspired by one and the same Spirit, who apportions to each one individually as he wills."

In Greek, the word for "gifts" is *charismata*, from which we get the much-used word "charismatic". In the last twenty years, the term has come to apply to specific Christians or churches who believe that these "gifts" are just as available today—to us—as they were to the first-century church.

I've never much liked the term "charismatic" as it's commonly used. The root word of *charismata* is *charis*, which means "grace". I agree with Donald Coggin, former archbishop of Canterbury, who said that the question is not whether a church is charismatic or non-charismatic. Why? Because if you understand the meaning of the word, all churches are charismatic; if a church doesn't live by God's gifts of grace, then it isn't a church—a club maybe, but not a church.

Manifestations for the Common Good

When speaking of the various ways the Holy Spirit chooses to make His ministering presence known, I prefer not to use the familiar phrase "the gifts of the Spirit," but instead the phrase Paul used immediately preceding the 1 Corinthians 12 list quoted above. He says there, "To each is given the manifestation of the Spirit for the common good," and then he enumerates them.

These manifestations, as Paul calls them, have come to be called gifts because the first verse of chapter 12 says, "Now concerning spiritual gifts, brethren, I do not want you to be uninformed." The old King James Version italicizes "gifts" in that sentence, as the word doesn't appear in the original Greek text. Instead, the Greek says, "Now concerning spirituals," "spirituals" being the plural noun.

There's something nice about that original Greek phrasing, as it helps reduce potential confusion on several accounts. First, we need all the semantic help we can muster to remind us that the Holy Spirit Himself is God's gift of grace—freely and equally given to all believers. Second, the English word "gifts" is often used synonymously with the lifelong talents or abilities of which we are called to be good stewards. Unlike our permanent talents, however, the manifestations of the Spirit are temporarily appropriated for a particular situation. God doesn't give us a manifestation and then expect us to "invest" it—or do anything at all with it, for that matter.

In one sense, however, the word "gift" is germane to the manifestations of the Spirit, and that sense can best be described in terms of a delivery person. Every day a paperman brings the newspaper to my front door. They aren't common anymore, but milkmen—and before that, icemen—used to make their rounds in most neighborhoods. Such functional names describe what people deliver—not what they make. In a similar way, when the Holy Spirit chooses to manifest Himself through my life, I become His deliveryman, bringing His *gift*—His wisdom or healing or faith—to someone else in the body of Christ.

Because the manifestation of healing affects the physical body of the person healed, it's probably the easiest manifestation to discuss in visual and understandable terms. One good example I know is the ministry of Francis MacNutt. Since 1967, the Holy Spirit has repeatedly chosen to heal people by manifesting Himself through that man. But Francis would be the first to say that he does not have the gift or talent to heal anybody.

He's only a channel through which a gift of healing is given to someone else. Whoever receives the manifestation is a carrier or a delivery person; the person who ultimately benefits from the manifestation receives the gift.

Suppose you're ill and a member of your Bible study prays for you. Then, either instantly (which sometimes happens) or over a period of time (which is more often the case), you're healed. *You* have received the gift of healing because the Holy Spirit chose to manifest Himself through your friend.

It's not unusual for the Holy Spirit repeatedly to manifest Himself in a particular way through a particular individual. When a recurring pattern becomes evident, we often say that such a person has a specific ministry, as did the late Kathryn Kuhlman. I'm said to have a ministry of teaching because the Holy Spirit repeatedly uses me as a channel to give His people gifts of knowledge and wisdom. Yet having that ministry does not make me knowledgeable or wise, nor does Francis MacNutt's ministry make him a healer. The ministries are powered by God, and that power is available to any yielded believer.

The various manifestations have characteristics in common. The 1 Corinthians 12 list begins and ends with blanket statements: "To each [person] is given the manifestation of the Spirit for the common good"; "All these [manifestations] are inspired by one and the same Spirit, who apportions to each one individually as he wills." From these two verses we can see God's purpose and method in giving the manifestations.

God wants to manifest Himself through the life of each and every believer. So the closer we as the body of

Christ get to that place where we're all delivering God's power, the closer we're getting to corporate spiritual health. Why? Because the Spirit manifests Himself for the "common good" or the common health.

The manifestations are given for the practical purpose of strengthening, building up and coordinating a group of believers. I don't think it's any accident that the remainder of chapter 12 goes into great detail describing the church as a physical body—with eyes, feet and ears—that must remain healthy and work together to function adequately and perform effectively.

Some people who have been baptized in the Holy Spirit are puzzled because they don't feel as though the Spirit is manifesting Himself through them. One possible reason for this is that it takes the body of Christ to receive the manifestations of the Spirit. With the exception of tongues, which we will discuss later, we're not given manifestations for our own sake, but for the sake of others.

This was true even in the life of Jesus. When He went back to His home town of Nazareth, He was unable to do any mighty works there because of their unbelief.[1] Now surely there was nothing wrong with Jesus. He was continuously and utterly yielded to the will of the Father; yet He was limited in what He could do because of the unbelief around Him.

If a body of Christians is unable or unwilling to receive the ministrations of the Spirit, He may not be able to show forth His presence through a believer, even though that person is ready and willing to be used as a channel. Because God manifests Himself only for the purpose of the common good, these visible effects of His presence should never be viewed as collectible merit badges in which we privately delight or publicly boast. Verse 11 makes it clear that the various manifestations are of the one Spirit and that He, not we, apportions them "as he wills." If He decides what manifestations occur, through whom, and when, we are not responsible for counting up how many we have so we can feel self-righteous or, on the other hand, so we can chastise ourselves for not being as spiritual as our neighbor.

This isn't the kind of situation where we're to look at our watch and say, "Heavens, it's 10:55 and I've already had a dozen manifestations of the Spirit today." It's possible, in fact, that we can deliver gifts without even being aware of our function. In a given day we may *know* that the Spirit has manifested Himself through us twice, but, in reality, He may have done so fifteen different times. We simply can't count up manifestations as stripes indicating our rank in the army of the Lord.

My wife and I both received the manifestation of tongues on the day we were baptized in the Holy Spirit. For several weeks we both prayed in the Spirit for a while in the evenings before going to bed. Then one night she received an interpretation. I was horrified! I thought, This is terrible. She has two manifestations and I have only one. The very idea!

But then, some time later, I prayed for someone and—to my astonishment—that person, who was ill, got better immediately. Ooooh, I was so excited, because *I* now had two spiritual badges—just like Ruth. Still later, I found myself offering an interpretation of tongues. My, how could I be so blessed!

I had no understanding of the basic principle that we all receive the same gift, the Holy Spirit. I didn't yet realize that only He can and does use us to manifest any one of the edifying evidences according to His will and the needs present at a specific time, in a specific place. The power to effect change in a person's life is God's to turn on, never ours. Francis MacNutt doesn't understand why God chooses to heal some people and not others through his ministry. Even Jesus or the apostles weren't given a power to heal which they could indiscriminately dispense.

Remember that Jesus once visited the pool of Bethesda, which was surrounded by paralytics and chronically sick people. Yet even He didn't heal everyone in sight, but rather only one man. I'm sure that if Francis MacNutt had the power to heal at his personal disposal he would spend night and day traveling from hospital to nursing home to hospice, sending everyone home—and not in wheelchairs. Francis knows, and we should always remember, that the Spirit always determines what gifts will be manifested and when.

With that in mind, let's look at several of the manifestations listed in 1 Corinthians 12 and discover a little bit more about how they work.

Wisdom and Knowledge

Although these are listed as two different manifestations, they're easiest to understand when they're defined in relation to each other. Knowledge is simply information. You might be on the telephone conversing with your sister, when she gives you a piece of information that's very important in helping you make a major decision. If that were to happen, you would have received a gift of knowledge, which the "carrier," the "utterer," may not have realized she was delivering.

Wisdom has more to do with insight, spiritual insight.

It's the light bulb drawn over the head of a cartoon character. For example, when I was a child I had a Sunday school teacher who couldn't have had more than an eighth-grade education. She'd never had any kind of biblical or theological training, yet her words were astoundingly profound and wise. When she spoke, God ministered gifts to people. I'm not sure she knew how God was using her, but that's not always important.

Sometimes I have no idea that something I've said has edified a particular individual. Yet there are other times when the Holy Spirit's manifestation of wisdom through me is God's gift to me. God often allows His wisdom to seep through the outgoing channel and into my own bloodstream.

One day a distraught woman came to me and asked a very direct question: "Where is this peace that passes understanding that you're always talking about?"

Immediately God struck me with the answer I was to give her. "The peace that passes understanding is found in the path of God's purpose for you." Right then and there I saw that the fruit of the Spirit grows in the garden of obedience and nowhere else. If we insist on walking outside of His will, the peace, joy, patience—the restfulness and at-easeness that slowly ripens in our lives—will wither on the vine.

That truth was not something any person had ever taught me; it wasn't a "line" I had up my sleeve in case such a question were asked.

It simply came from the Holy Spirit to minister to this needy woman who later acknowledged that she had found understanding—and to myself as well, who more clearly saw how the Holy Spirit grows all His fruit in our lives.

Faith

It's important that we look at this particular manifestation because the word "faith" is also listed in Galatians 5 as one of the fruit of the Spirit. Why? Because there are two different kinds of faith a believer can have.

The faith that's a fruit of the Spirit grows and matures in a Christian's life. But the faith that's a manifestation has a temporary and extraordinary nature; it comes upon a person so that he or she can accomplish a certain task.

One of the most dramatic Bible stories illustrating this second kind of faith is found in the Old Testament book of 1 Kings.[2] (Remember, there's nothing exclusively "New Testament" about the Holy Spirit coming upon people and giving them temporary power for a specific purpose. But since Pentecost, these manifestations are available to all believers, not just a select few.)

Scripture describes Elijah as a human—just like the rest of us. Yet he took on an amazing challenge: He said that his God was capable of sending down fire from heaven. On Mount Carmel he had a huge altar built. Two bulls were slaughtered for sacrifice, but nobody was allowed to bring any matches. The 450 prophets of Baal and 400 prophets of Asherah were to call on their god. Elijah was to call on his, and, as Elijah said, "The God who answers by fire, he is God."

Elijah let the priests go first. He stood back and watched their wild incantations. When nothing happened, the priests grew more feverish, cutting themselves with knives. Finally Elijah gave them a little jab, saying, "Cry a little louder. Maybe your god is on a journey, or maybe he's asleep and needs to be wakened."

Hours later, Elijah took his turn. He tidied up the

altar, then added a little Cecil B. DeMille touch: He had them dig a trench around the altar and douse the meat and wood with water three times—until the moat was full. Then Elijah stepped up, prayed two long sentences, and pow!—the fire fell and consumed the offering, the wood, the stones, the dust, even the water. Now that took *some* faith.

Then we read in the next chapter that the queen, who had introduced Baal worship to the Israelite people in the first place, was furious. She said, "Elijah, by this time tomorrow you're a dead man."

How did Elijah, this great man of faith, react? He ran away in terror. He had enough faith to call fire down from heaven, yet he was afraid of a queen's threats on his life. So what happened? I believe that such extraordinary faith was not his constant possession, but was God's way of showing Himself to other people.

Both kinds of faith are important in a Christian's life. But the kind of faith that effects great miracles is not one that gradually grows, and—as with any of God's power—it will never be appropriated except to accomplish God's purposes.

The Ability to Distinguish Between Spirits

Discernment is the ability to understand what is from God and what is not. Whatever is not of God is not necessarily of Satan—it could be of the flesh. Malachi prophesies about this manifestation in the chapter 3, verse 18: "Then once more shall you distinguish between the righteous and the wicked, between one who serves God and one who does not serve him." Jesus Himself manifested this particular gift. It's recorded in the last verse of the second chapter of John that "he knew all men and needed no one to bear witness of man, for he himself knew what was in man.''

Discernment might well be called a fruit as well as a manifestation of the Spirit, for as the Word and the will of the Lord become more a part of a person's life, sin and error tend to stand out more sharply in contrast. Discernment presupposes that we have a deep desire to do God's will in a given situation, an openness to His way, paved with an experiential knowledge of Him. Thus Paul speaks in Ephesians 6 of ''putting on the whole armor of God,'' which is an image of active, thorough preparation to do the will of God.

Discernment as manifested in action depends upon the presence of certain qualities in a person. Humility, charity and courage must be present in an attitude of submission. Humility is essential because situations of faith require full dependence upon God. We need discernment most in obscure situations, when we face roadblocks. But if we're too proud to be guided, it's not likely that we'll be used to manifest this particular grace. Charity must also be present, and I use that word rather than ''love'' to illustrate a particular lack of any judgment involved. I've seen people ''speak the truth in love'' when there wasn't a bit of charity involved! Charity implies our bending over to be gracious to another, being completely devoid of judgment—which gets in the way of true discernment.

True discernment occurs in an absence of self, which is hard to achieve. We all tend to have our agendas for others. Even Peter was told that he couldn't know of Jesus' plans for John; when he asked the Lord, he was told to mind his own business.[3] This aspect of discernment is not to be treated lightly.

We had an incident in our parish recently when judgment was practiced rather than true discernment. Two of the women who were on a prayer team thought God had spoken to them concerning a person with whom they'd prayed. They were in an excited state when they came to the office and described the situation, naming the sins they'd encountered. Gentle prodding established the identity of the person for whom they'd prayed. It turned out that the person was in no way capable of being possessed of such spirits, nor of comprehending their prayer, but was one who would remain a child for the duration of her life on earth. They had misinterpreted the person's actions, and judgment had interrupted the channels through which discernment might have flowed.

Courage, of course, must be present as well, because risks are involved. If you're discerning direction for yourself, you'll need courage to follow. If you're discerning a message for others, you'll need courage to tell them! Either way, you'll want to be certain before you speak or act.

Discernment functions only in an atmosphere of prayer. Thomas Green calls discernment "where prayer and action meet." I started out by describing it as a feeling process, because that's the way it most often manifests itself. You can feel God's will (its presence or absence) without understanding it with the mind, and feel an urgency to respond in obedience.

A scriptural picture of true discernment in action is the agony of Jesus in Gethsemane. When He said, "Father, not my will, but yours be done," He was in prayer. He had submitted His own understanding and asked whether the cup might be taken from Him. Full of humility, He saw that Calvary was the only road; and *that* act of charity took great courage.

Paul, in 1 Corinthians 14, goes into great detail discussing three of the manifestations—prophecy, tongues and the related interpretation of tongues. Because Paul had so much to say about these evidences of the Spirit, I also want to look at them more closely in the next chapter.

Chapter Ten

Mouthpiece and Mystery

Apparently, several of the verbal manifestations—prophecy, tongues and the interpretation of tongues—were cause for some confusion in the Corinthian church. Paul wanted Christians there—and for centuries to come—to have some clarity on what part these manifestations were to have in public worship services. As you can see if you read 1 Corinthians 14, these evidences of the Spirit are interrelated, but before we weave them together, let's look at them separately.

Prophecy

A prophet is not someone who gazes into a crystal ball and predicts the future. In very succinct terms, a prophet is and always has been a mouthpiece or spokesman for God. Prophecy has more to do with forthtelling than with foretelling.

I can best illustrate the meaning of prophet by relating a little more of the story of Moses at the burning bush.

You may remember that Moses would not accept God's offer of heightened verbal skills, and that God got angry and went to a contingency plan: Moses' older brother, Aaron, was to be the public speaker in Moses' stead. God said to Moses, "[Aaron] shall speak for you to the people; and he shall be a mouth for you, and you shall be to him as God."[1] This ended up being a clumsy relationship—God speaking to Moses who spoke to Aaron who spoke to Pharaoh and the people.

Exodus 7:1-2 describes this Moses-Aaron relationship in realistic terms. God, speaking to Moses, said, "Aaron your brother shall be your prophet. You shall speak all that I command you; and Aaron your brother shall tell Pharaoh to let the people of Israel go out of his land." Aaron was Moses' prophet, his mouthpiece. In a sense, Moses put words into Aaron's mouth. And God, intangible and invisible as He is, can and does speak to the church through the lips of fallible human beings.

Never has there been a time when this manifestation was needed more than it is today. Yes, we have the Word of God as it is presented in Scripture, but God also has a contemporary word for us. Although it will never contradict the written Word, God is ready and willing to enlighten His people by speaking through the lips of His spokesmen and women.

Second Peter 1:20-21 speaks directly to this issue, giving an even clearer perspective on God's speaking through humankind: "First of all you must understand this, that no prophecy of Scripture is a matter of one's own interpretation, because no prophecy ever came by the impulse of man, but men moved by the Holy Spirit spoke from God."

Of course, this possibility—that the Holy Spirit can and does manifest Himself by empowering someone to speak forth His own words—raises some significant problems. This particular blend of the human and the divine is such that a great deal of error can creep in. Because the Holy Spirit does not anesthetize a person's own mind or mouth and "drive" him or her to speak words of the Lord, there is always a possibility that the human spirit might add to or even invent visions of its own mind. With this manifestation of the Holy Spirit and corresponding gift, more than with any of the others, we must be careful to discern, judge and test the rightness of the words.

In 1 Corinthians 14, when Paul gives instructions for the functioning of the local church meeting, he says, "Let two or three prophets speak, and let the others weigh what is said."[2] We are told not to assume that every word spoken in the Lord's name is from the Holy Spirit. It's difficult to judge the authenticity of every message, but both the Old and New Testaments give us some criteria for discerning prophetic words.

First, 1 John 4:1-3 gives a basic and broad measure: "Do not believe every spirit, but test the spirits to see whether they are of God; for many false prophets have gone out into the world. By this you know the Spirit of God: every spirit which confesses that Jesus Christ has come in the flesh is of God, and every spirit which does not confess Jesus is not of God."

When discerning whether or not a person is speaking for God, this compact rule can be your first guideline. A person who says, "Well, Jesus was a great prophet, the founder of one of the great religions, a great teacher," isn't speaking lies, but neither is he or she saying enough about who Jesus was. The same is true of a person who talks about God without naming Jesus as the Son of God incarnate, as the center of the faith. A person who doesn't confess Jesus' divinity surely isn't manifesting the Holy Spirit, although the Scriptures mention other ways to test specific prophetic pronouncements.

In the 1 Corinthians 14 passage, Paul reminds us that God always works "decently and in order." He's a gentleman who doesn't interrupt or disrupt or cause confusion in a group of people. Just as He doesn't anesthetize a spokesman's mind, He doesn't motorize his or her mouth. Verse 32 says, "The spirits of the prophets are subject to the prophets," meaning that God's Spirit within you doesn't just overpower your spirit, but is subject to your spirit. Anyone who says, "I can't help myself; I've got to say this right now," isn't moving in the Spirit, but is being driven by his or her own impulses. The work of the Spirit has a peaceful quality that is the very opposite of drivenness.

False Prophecy

What are other indications that someone's words are not from the Holy Spirit? In Jeremiah 23:16-17 the Lord gives two criteria for false prophecy. He says, "Do not listen to the words of the prophets who prophesy to you, filling you with vain hopes; they speak visions of their own minds, not from the mouth of the Lord. They say continually to those who despise the word of the Lord, 'It shall be well with you'; and to every one who stubbornly follows his own heart, they say, 'No evil shall come upon you.' "

What's the effect of those who claim to be but really aren't speaking under the Lord's anointing? They encourage people in their rebellion. False prophets say whatever people want to hear. They say, "Go ahead. Do your own thing. It doesn't matter, because everybody's doing it and, besides, God is really a loving, indulgent grandfather—fortunately a little deaf and blind." This kind of talk has a steady audience because people love to be assured that their own plans are all right with God.

False prophecy nearly always encourages people to follow their own way and to turn from the voice of the Lord, while true prophecy calls believers to repentance—though never in a condemning fashion. Paul makes it clear that "he who prophesies speaks to men for their upbuilding and encouragement and consolation."[3]

Although it may not at first seem obvious, a prophet can call for repentance in a consoling and encouraging way. No matter how dire the predictions of disaster spoken through the Old Testament Hebrew prophets, they were always accompanied by the word of God's mercy and grace. I've heard prophecies presented in the name of the Lord that covered a crowd with a fog of discouragement, and when that's happened my spirit has known that the words were not of God.

We have from time to time had persons who've spoken out in worship in words that are disturbingly out of step with the witness of Scripture. I've found it necessary to respond to these "prophecies" by reminding the congregation that Scripture says such-and-such in such a place, as a gentle correction. Though the person may have spoken earnestly, believing the word was from the Lord, our God does not contradict Himself! And we must allow room for stumbling as the gifts are manifested among us.

I'll also get letters with "the word of the Lord" to me or to the congregation that are often rambling and non-specific. But I believe that God doesn't leave us guessing! At other times I might get messages that could be words from the Lord, but they have only rebuke and not redirection in them. The Holy Spirit doesn't tear down without building up, so I wait until the message is complete before taking action on them. These may come from sincere people of deep faith, but the Lord hasn't manifested this gift if it comes out in this way. The messages they have passed along are from another source, most likely their own opinions or concerns.

But why don't false prophets speak the Word? Verse 18 of Jeremiah 23 gives an explanation: "For who among them has stood in the council of the Lord to perceive and to hear his word, or who has given heed to his word and listened?" Although the word used in this verse is "council"—as in a group of people sitting around a board room making decisions—I don't think we do the verse injustice if we substitute the word "counsel"—the advice found in the Scriptures and within our own hearts. False prophets don't quiet themselves and stand before the Lord long enough to hear the whispers of the Spirit.

The Lord goes on to describe further the false prophets by saying, "I did not send the [false] prophets, yet they ran; I did not speak to them, yet they prophesied. But if they had stood in my council, then they would have proclaimed my words to my people, and they would have turned them from their evil way, and from the evil of their doings."[4] If we read between the lines and, from these verses, try to identify a characteristic of a true prophet, we can see that the Holy Spirit speaks through those who make a practice of taking the time to listen to the voice of God—who rarely speaks hurriedly.

This process of waiting on God and hearing His words fills a prophet with a divine energy that can quickly be identified as having authority. A true prophetic word often has a "thus saith the Lord" quality that obviously is not typical of the speaker in his or her own right. This was true of the thundering Old Testament prophets and surely of John the Baptist. The Gospels say that the people of Jesus' day knew that His teaching was more authoritative than that of the scribes and Pharisees.

Receiving Prophecy

Something about a true prophetic utterance calls for action and draws people toward God. Yet at the same time, it's never a prophet's place to go around saying, "The Lord has told me to give you this heavy message." The *hearer* of the word must always discern the truth of the words.

Further on in Jeremiah 23, the Lord compares true prophecies with false by saying, "What has straw in common with wheat?...Is not my word like fire...and like a hammer which breaks the rock in pieces...? Behold, I am against the prophets...who use their tongues and say, 'Says the Lord.' "[5]

The rest of that chapter is somewhat difficult to understand, but it points out that the word of the Lord, when spoken forth, stands on its own and speaks for itself. This insight is confirmed by a wonderful little verse hidden away in Luke: "Wisdom [or truth] is justified by all her children."[6] It stands the test of time, and it's powerful. If the Lord tells me to speak forth a certain utterance, I'm called to be obedient, to say the words; but then I must leave the acceptance of it in God's hands.

As with the other manifestations we've discussed, it's possible that a person receiving the manifestation may not know the needs his or her words are addressing, and the message may be a "gift hammer" to only one person out of many who are present. Several years ago I accompanied Dr. and Mrs. Charles Hummel of Inter-Varsity Christian Fellowship (he's a well-known author) to a large church gathering. Arriving a little early, we sat in the car awhile before we went in, and while waiting, he told me of a particular problem he faced. He had no idea which way to turn and he asked for prayer.

Right there in the car we asked God for guidance and then walked into the meeting. In the course of the evening all of the manifestations of the Spirit occurred, including a prophecy that couldn't possibly have applied to any situation other than Dr. Hummel's. He heard it and instantly recognized it as God's word to him, as did his wife and I. We all knew that God had answered our prayer, but the person who spoke that prophecy couldn't have had a clue as to what it meant or for whom it had been given.

Isn't it wonderful to have a God who works in such mysterious ways to fulfill His purposes through His children—and in His children?

In His amazing plan, God channels the living water within us outward to edify other people. But He also allows for an amazing "short-circuited" channel through which He can and does build up the person through whom He's manifesting Himself. That channel is the manifestation of tongues.

Tongues

First Corinthians 14:4 says, "He who speaks in a tongue edifies himself," and this manifestation is the only one given for the purpose of strengthening the one through whom it flows. In this case, the one receiving the manifestation also receives the gift—of being purified, built up and cleaned up. (It's as if a milkman delivered milk to himself.)

The Greek word which we translate as "tongues" is *glossa*, which means "foreign tongues". If I speak in tongues, I speak in a language that I haven't learned, as one does a second language such as Spanish or French. The foreign tongue is a language given to me by the Holy Spirit.

In a word, tongues is prayer. It's my spirit (or your spirit) communicating with God's Spirit in a language understood by both spirits, but not by my mind. I love the phrase often used to describe speaking in tongues— "prayer in the spirit." Paul describes it by saying that we're uttering "mysteries in the Spirit."[7] Later on he describes the mystery this way: "For if I pray in a tongue, my spirit prays but my mind is unfruitful."[8]

Your first question might be, "If you don't know what you're saying, how can it possibly benefit you?" Such a question betrays a prejudice—that we can only benefit from what we can rationally understand, and that truth must be filtered through intellect.

It's impossible for me to explain exactly how this spiritual process happens, just as it's impossible for me to explain exactly how pork chops and broccoli and ice cream become my hair and skin and blood. Yet that physical process which takes place deep within my body is no more real than the spiritual process which takes place deep within my spirit.

Tongues is by far the most controversial of the manifestations, probably because it's the one most baffling to our intellects. This manifestation and gift have been absent from the central life of the Western church for several long periods of time, not because the Spirit was inactive, but because a pervading intellectualism froze the activity.

When I was in the Sinai I visited the world's oldest Christian monastery—St. Catherine's. Since their establishment in the second century, this group has experienced an unbroken tradition of the free operation of all the manifestations, including tongues. This continual outpouring is much more common in the Eastern churches than in the West, and because the organized Roman or Protestant churches didn't see this as central to their experience, theologians gradually rationalized the manifestation's absence. Despite Paul's clear statement, "Now I want you all to speak in tongues,"[9] despite his insistence that "God has appointed in the church...speakers in various kinds of tongues," some people choose to justify the position that this manifestation has no place in these modern times.

I admire one noted evangelical leader, Harold Ockenga, for years pastor of Park Street Church in Boston and first president of Fuller Theological Seminary. At one time he took a strong stand against the manifestation of tongues. Then one by one his board of deacons was baptized in the Holy Spirit; they received the gift of tongues. Ockenga had previously held such a firm position on this subject that he knew he had to respond in one of two ways: by saying these people were completely deluded or by admitting that he was wrong.

He says that it was a great struggle for him. He wanted to maintain his position, but he couldn't ignore or deny the godly fruit that grew out of these people's lives. As he allowed God to break down the cold rationalism of his theology, he acknowledged the reality of the spontaneous operation of the Holy Spirit. It takes a big man to say, "I will change my theology rather than deny the Word of God."

I don't think anyone is more aware than I of how strange it may sound for people living on the edge of the twenty-first century to be talking about a manifestation that by-passes the intellect. I'm acutely aware that our Christian faith is a rational one. But I also know that, just as some dimensions of life aren't accessible to our senses, some dimensions of life aren't accessible to our intellects. I've never seen an atom, yet I believe the scientists who tell me that the universe—even my own body—is made of them. We don't have to see something to know it's real, and we don't have to understand something to experience it.

Why would God make this kind of communication possible? If our prayer lives were limited by our intellects, we really wouldn't know exactly what to pray for. Think of your mind as a funnel. Your intellect is the little hole at the bottom. Imagine how much of God's refreshing water can pour through to edify you if He by-passes the restricting hole at the bottom of the funnel and communicates directly with your spirit. God's ways are so much bigger than we can comprehend.

Romans 8:26-28 says, "We do not know how to pray as we ought, but the Spirit himself intercedes for us with sighs too deep for words....The Spirit intercedes for the saints according to the will of God."

We never possess all the facts in a situation; we "see through a glass darkly." But when we pray in the Spirit, the Spirit utters the words that are acceptable and pleasing to God and always in accordance with His will.

Of course God understands English, but our vocabularies are limited by what we've been taught or how well we've read the dictionaries. For example, if I want to worship God, I could say, "I worship You; I praise You; I adore You; I magnify You; I extol You." Those are all the English words I know to express that thought. We're not only confined by our inability to see the big picture, but also by our few words.

Because tongues is prayer, it most frequently takes place in private. Prayer is designed for the ears of the Lord, and in this most personal communication between you and God, your love and praise and worship and concern are expressed more deeply than you can understand.

Because tongues is the only manifestation for our own personal edification, it's the only one over which we have control; we can pray in the Spirit at will, any time, day or night, under any circumstances. It's as natural and effortless for me to pray in the Spirit as it is for me to speak in English. Why? Because it's always God's will for us to be edified or built up. It's always His will for us to commune with Him. Ephesians 6:18 instructs us to "pray at all times in the Spirit, with all prayer and supplication."

I'm often asked how a person receives this manifestation and gift. If God wants His people to be built up, this gift is available to anyone who is yielded to His purposes. Many people, however, have simply never appropriated this manifestation.

Suppose that I hid a ten-dollar bill in a secret compartment of my wallet and then forgot that I'd put it there. If six months later I were to run out of gas at a most inopportune time—after I'd been to the store and before I'd gone to the bank—I'd look in my wallet and panic that I had no money. The hidden ten dollars would be there, but it would be of no use to me. I would go through all the agonies of being stranded penniless, even though my help was right in my hand.

The same sort of thing can happen with the manifestation of a prayer language. It's available to us, but it can be hidden from us. God never forces someone to speak in tongues. Demonic spirits may possess people and control them with an iron fist, but the Holy Spirit fills us and frees us.

Throughout history, miracles often have been preceded by a human's natural act. As a person steps out in evidence of faith, God responds. You might remember that Moses had to throw down his rod before it turned into a snake; he had to pick up the snake before it turned back into a rod. Joshua had to marshall his troops and march around Jericho seven days before the city fell.

This same principle works when a believer wants to receive the gift of tongues. As evidence of your faith, you have to do something: You have to start speaking. As you speak, God gives the utterance.

Have you ever tried to steer a parked car? The wheels on an immobile vehicle might turn, but a car has to be moving if it's going to be guided.

In a similar way, a person has to be speaking if he or she is going to talk. If we do our share, if we step out in faith, God will meet us halfway and manifest Himself.

My Own Experience

My own manifestation of tongues came after years of suspicion that anything of the sort could be of God. When I was a teenager, my brother and I had gone to spy on a Pentecostal "camp meeting" that took place near where I grew up. I remember that we drove through the gate of the place where the meeting was held and turned the car around, aiming it out in case we had to make a quick getaway! We couldn't see the people from where we had parked the car, because there was a little rise in the hill, so we got out and climbed the hill and peered over it into the natural amphitheater below where the meeting was taking place. I couldn't believe my eyes!

I had never seen anything like it—hundreds of people singing and shouting, waving their hands in the air. In the church of my childhood, we knelt and prayed quietly! To me, the Pentecostal experience was the lunatic fringe of the ecclesiastical realm, and that prejudice stayed with me for quite a while.

Time passed. I grew up, went to the Eastman School of Music in Rochester, New York, and while there served as an organist and choir director of a large Methodist church. The pastor of that church gave me a book one day, entitled *Deeper Experiences of Famous Christians*. It told the stories of some of the people God has used to change the course of history, and I read the book with interest.

All of those people in the book said they had had an experience with God, sometimes years after their initial conversion, in which they found the power of the Christian experience in life. John Wesley called it "entire sanctification." Others spoke of it as a "second blessing" or "baptism of love," and yet others used the expression "the baptism in the Spirit."

It was clear to me that however they described it, they were all talking about the same thing—and I had not experienced it. God used that little book to create in me a profound hunger for a deeper touch of His Spirit in my life. I knew I was a Christian—I had accepted Jesus and been accepted by Him. I was serving Him, yet I was aware that a number of things in my life were out of harmony with the will of God, and I wasn't able to do anything about them. I prayed, confessed, but nothing seemed to work.

I often thought to myself as I looked around at the congregation on a Sunday that if other people didn't have more of an experience of God than I had, it was amazing that the church had lasted as long as it had. I was raised on Scripture and knew it contained a description of life that didn't bear much resemblance to what I was experiencing, or to what others I knew had experienced, even though we were Christians.

Finally the evening came when I said to the Lord, "Tonight's the night! We've got to settle this thing once and for all." I went upstairs with my Bible, discreetly pulled down the window shades and locked the door, and got down on my knees.

I said, "Whatever You want to do in my life, that's what I want." I began to review my whole life. I went back as far as I could go, confessing every sin I could think of—and even some I had imagined! I took every earthly possession I had (you can be sure it wasn't much!) and systematically offered them to the Lord. I promised Him that I would commit to Him every day of my life from that moment on, if only He would give me whatever it was I needed. I prayed throughout the whole night. I know that never in my life was there a moment—before or since—when I have been more yielded and open to the Lord.

But whatever it was I expected, it simply didn't occur. When I finally got up from my knees, I began to rationalize the absence of any manifestation of a particular experience with God: "Well, maybe I'm not old enough. Maybe I'm not good enough." (I had some knowledge of the grace of God and really didn't think that was the problem, but I was rationalizing!)

I finally concluded that God just didn't want to do anything, and that was all there was to it. So I said to the Almighty, "Now, Lord, remember this day. Don't forget it, because I met You more than half way tonight. I just want You to remember, if You're ever not satisfied with my life, that it's Your fault, because You didn't give me whatever it was I needed."

You may think that's presumptuous, but that's how I felt, and since we deal with a God before whom all hearts are open, all desires known, and from whom no secrets are hid, I felt I might as well tell Him! I felt then and for some time after that night that I had done absolutely everything I knew how to do to prepare myself for whatever He might have wanted to do, and I concluded since nothing happened that He didn't want to do anything!

This was a bit of a blow to my ego, but it didn't destroy my faith. I didn't go storming out of the church; I remained faithfully in it and continued my musical education. I simply told the Lord that I was going to forget about it: "Now, Lord, I just can't think about this anymore. It's been consuming too much of my time, and I did what I could, and You didn't do what You should, and so I'm putting it out of my mind."

Eventually I felt that my musical education, though interesting and inspiring, was a bit one-sided. I became interested in philosophy and decided to major in philosophy. I started all over again, went another four years, then enrolled in Harvard Graduate School for a master's program in philosophy, took a lot of theology and psychology and all sorts of things, went to Boston University for a couple of more years after that, and was educated far beyond my intelligence! This was compatible with my personality, for I'm an ivory-tower kind of person.

Then I took a teaching job at a small Christian college in Rhode Island and became organist/choirmaster of a very fine Episcopal church. One day, the rector called me and said, "Terry, what are you doing tonight?"

Because I knew him rather well, I responded, "Why?"

He said, "There's a man who's coming to speak at one of the motels, and he's going to stay with us at the rectory. An emergency has come up, and we can't be there. Could you and Ruth go, and after the meeting bring him back?"

I asked, "Who's the man?" And he answered, "The Rev. Dennis Bennett of St. Mark's, Van Nuys, California."

I knew a bit about Dennis Bennett because *Newsweek* just a few weeks before had devoted their whole religion section to what had happened at his church. I could hardly believe that the things *Newsweek* reported could happen in any Episcopal church, so I said, "I'd love to go!"

I'd never seen anybody who was filled with the Holy
Spirit, which is what this man was reported to be. I
didn't know if their faces would shine or fire would
come from their eyes or what! So we made our way
to the hotel, and I was more than a bit curious. We found
ourselves among 275 or so others, mostly clergy. I was
not ordained at the time and had not even thought of
it, but I knew many of the people there, and I felt a bit
more secure.

When Bennett walked through the door, my heart
sank. Now he's not a bad-looking man; some might
think him handsome. But he had a crew cut! This didn't
fit my image of a Spirit-filled man, and my reaction was,
"Can any good thing come out of Van Nuys?"

But that was before he started to speak. He didn't
preach; he just talked for an hour and twenty minutes,
and related the story of his church and his experience.
As he spoke, I found I had lots of questions I wanted
to ask him when he got into the car. When he came to
the end of his talk, he said, "Tonight, if there's anybody
here who would like to be baptized in the Holy Spirit,
we've secured a suite of rooms on the second floor and
we would invite you to come up and pray with us. We
will receive the Holy Spirit in the Episcopal way"—
which, to me, meant decently and in order!

At the moment he dismissed us, a couple we hadn't
seen for over a year came up to us and said, "Do you
know what happened to us?" We knew them to be
Christians, fairly quiet Christians; the man was a con-
cert violinist with the Boston Symphony Orchestra. We
replied that we had no idea what had happened to them,
and they proceeded to regale us with the way they and
their children had been baptized in the Holy Spirit and

what a difference it had made in their lives. The wife looked me straight in the eye and said, "Have you been baptized in the Holy Spirit?" I said, "No."

I realized that I could have given that woman a lecture on the Holy Spirit. I could have taken her on a week's worth of Bible study on the subject; but that wasn't what she asked me. I knew that in the sense of her question and the sense of Dennis Bennett's experience, I had not been baptized in the Spirit.

She replied, "I rather think you will be, very soon." I told her, "Well, I'm willing, if He wants to..." and immediately was reminded of the time years before when I had spent a whole night asking the Lord for something very much like what she was describing— but to no avail. The Lord hadn't done anything for me then, and I couldn't see anything different in my life now, so I saw no reason at all why He should choose this time over that one.

We were a bit late getting to the "upper room." We found Bennett in the corner and perhaps 35 people gathered in the two rooms. He was explaining a few things as we came through the door. He said, "Now I'm going to lay hands on you and pray for you. You must understand that the power won't come dripping out of my shoulders through my hands onto your shoulders. I lay hands on you simply following the example of the apostles. Jesus is the baptizer in the Holy Spirit, not me."

So far, I had no problem. Then he said, "What I want you to do, after I pray for you, is to turn your whole heart unto the Lord and begin to pray to Him, but not in English."

You cannot imagine the feeling that came over me

in that moment. In his talk when he had mentioned "speaking in tongues," the idea had been to me about as acceptable as swinging from a chandelier! I had had years and years of study in psychology (most of it abnormal psychology) and I wasn't the least bit interested in manifesting this particular behavior.

So with a fair amount of courage, I raised my hand and said, "Father Bennett, I am very interested in what you're calling the baptism in the Spirit, but frankly, I'm not much interested in this tongues business." He smiled benignly and said, "Many times it comes with the package!" Somehow I felt that I was not called upon to instruct him at that point.

Bennett started praying with the person on his right. I knew the man: He was a well-educated, seemingly balanced pastor of a large church and had a respectable ministry. To my astonishment, this man began to pray in what seemed to me to be a completely articulate language. I strained to hear him, but of course, he wasn't speaking to me. Bennett went on to the next one and then the next, and it was like dominoes—they were all having similar experiences!

My wife and I were positioned inside the door of the second room, and as Bennett got closer to me, I got more and more frightened. I prayed, "Lord, I'm not here for some weird experience, especially You-know-what, but if there's something You have that could help me to love You more perfectly and serve You more effectively, then I would like it." As I recall that evening, I think I was afraid that nothing would happen, since nothing had happened previously.

When Bennett got to where we were kneeling at the corner of a bed, he stopped for a moment, then walked by and started on the other side of the room. I knew then the feeling of a convict reprieved at the last minute from the electric chair. I felt I had a little while left. Finally, he closed in from the other side and prayed for my wife, Ruth, first. Then he got to me and said, "Lord Jesus, baptize this, Your very *fearful* servant, in Your Spirit." That's all he said.

I didn't see any tongues of fire, hear any mighty, rushing wind or feel any warm slushy feeling in my heart. I was a bit more relaxed at the absence of such phenomena, until he said, "Now turn your heart to the Lord, and praise Him, but not in English."

That was the closest I have ever come to a cardiac arrest. He was asking me to do something I didn't want to do, that I had never wanted to do and that I couldn't see any purpose in (at least not for an Episcopalian—it didn't seem decent or orderly). The only memory I'd had of anything like that before this night was that evening when I'd discovered I like to do things in a more seemly fashion than those who seemed to me to be dancing and working themselves into a frenzy, shooting off into orbit. I had spent years after that childhood experience studying how to think and how to speak what I was thinking, so that it would come out right. But now it sounded to me as if Bennett were asking me to put my brain in neutral, my tongue in high gear, and step on the gas!

It was the hardest thing I've ever done in my life. But God gave me grace. I felt like a fool, but I took a deep breath and started in. To my complete astonishment, words poured effortlessly from my mouth, completely by-passing my mind; they came right from the heart. I only had to make a sound or two in my own strength before God freed His power within me and gave me access to a prayer language. When I acted, God responded. When I turned my thoughts toward praise and worship and uttered sounds that made no sense to me, God released the spirit-to-Spirit communication that was beyond my intellectual understanding.

Tongues in the Public Meeting

Although most speaking in tongues occurs in private and is as natural as breathing, the Spirit sometimes moves upon a person to speak forth in an unknown tongue in a public meeting. Unlike the private and personal prayer in the Spirit, this use of the manifestation is not ours to instigate, and the Holy Spirit doesn't manifest Himself this way through every believer.

At the end of 1 Corinthians 12, Paul asks a series of questions: "Are all apostles? Are all prophets? Are all teachers? Do all work miracles? Do all possess gifts of healing? Do all speak with tongues? Do all interpret?"[10] Although Paul doesn't actually answer the questions, the implied response is no. It's important here to see that he is referring to the *public* manifestation of tongues. *All* may privately pray in the Spirit, but not all are moved to speak in a foreign tongue in public.

At the same time, this manifestation isn't a luxury, a fringe benefit or an option in a vital church's life. Again, Paul says, "And God has appointed in the church first apostles, second prophets, third teachers, then workers of miracles, then healers, helpers, administrators, speakers in various kinds of tongues."[11] He makes it pretty obvious that God has appointed some in the church to speak in tongues. Right alongside the distinguished ministry of the apostles, the prophets, the teachers, the administrators, there is a particular ministry of speaking in tongues. If such ministries are God-appointed, they are necessary for the full ordering of the church as God would like it to be.

Prophecy and Tongues in Worship

As I said at the beginning of this chapter, the public manifestations of prophecy and tongues are interrelated and discussed by Paul at great length in 1 Corinthians 14. We've already looked at a few of the verses; they helped us define the manifestations. But let's look now at the beginning of this passage and pinpoint the relationship between these two.

"Make love your aim, and earnestly desire the spiritual gifts, especially that you may prophesy. For one who speaks in a tongue speaks not to men but to God; for no one understands him, but he utters mysteries in the Spirit. On the other hand, he who prophesies speaks to men for their upbuilding and for their upbuilding and encouragement and consolation. He who speaks in a tongue edifies himself, but he who prophesies edifies the church. Now I want you all to speak in tongues, but even more to prophesy. He who prophesies is greater than he who speaks in tongues, unless some one interprets, so that the church may be edified. Now, brethren, if I come to you speaking in tongues, how shall I benefit you unless I bring you some revelation or knowledge of prophecy or teaching?"

The first verse, "Desire the spiritual gifts, especially that you may prophesy," points out there *is* a place for what I call spiritual ambition. Not personal ambition that pits one person against another in a competition of self-righteousness, but a godly ambition that flows forth from our eagerness to be used by God to equip the body of Christ for the task that is laid upon them.

In a public meeting prophecy is more important than tongues, because prophecy edifies the whole group. There's something exclusive about the personal nature of the Spirit-to-spirit communication of tongues. Whenever a language is spoken that I don't understand, I'm an outsider, a foreigner. If you're speaking in such a language, I become an observer rather than a participator.

But the Holy Spirit manifests Himself in yet another way, by giving someone an interpretation of a prayer spoken in a foreign tongue. This interpretation is not a translation of the unintelligible words that have been spoken. Whenever one speaks in tongues he or she is speaking to God and the words are addressed to God; an interpretation is always addressed to a group of people. God takes the concern of the prayer in tongues and, in turn, gives His word on that issue to the group as a whole. I can best describe how this works by giving an example.

A number of years ago I was asked to speak to nearly three thousand people gathered at the Hilton Hotel in New York City. The audience was predominantly Protestant, people who attended nonliturgical evangelical churches. After I spoke, a Roman Catholic priest gave a powerful testimony. This was before the Holy Spirit had moved upon and renewed the Catholic Church as He has in the last ten years, and this priest was one of the first American Catholics to have received the baptism of the Holy Spirit.

The moment this man finished and sat down, someone else stood up and started to speak in tongues in a most calm, natural way, and immediately the convention hall went silent. It was as if the Spirit Himself hushed the audience. This man didn't speak in tongues very long—

just a few seconds—and then another man got up and gave an interpretation, which was addressed to the "congregation." The words were spoken with so much authority that they've been burned into my memory: "My children, why are you surprised at what you have seen and heard? Did I not say I would pour out My Spirit on all flesh? These divisions are your divisions; they are not My divisions."

As I see the situation, the Spirit was grieved by the self-righteous attitude of the group that had listened to the priest's testimony. No one said it, of course, but we could read the faces in the congregation: "Isn't it wonderful that this poor benighted Roman Catholic has, at last, seen the truth."

Someone sensitive to the Spirit was used of the Lord to voice a prayer about this particular sin, and another was used to bring the matter to our attention. At the end of that meeting, there was a wonderful unity in that hall, a common understanding that we'd heard the word of the Lord, and that He'd been displeased. We'd been chastised—though not condemned.

Whenever a person feels led to pray in the Spirit aloud in front of a group, that person and the group as a whole should expect that God will give an interpretation, either to someone else or to the original speaker, so that everyone may be edified. Occasionally someone at St. Paul's will speak forth in tongues, and when this happens we immediately pray that the Lord will give us an interpretation—which He always does. If, by some chance, He didn't, it wouldn't be a scandal; it would simply indicate that no one else should speak forth in a foreign tongue.

Verses 26-33 give more insight into these manifestations as they're used by God in worship services:

"When you come together, each one has a hymn, a lesson, a revelation, a tongue, or an interpretation. Let all things be done for edification. If any speak in a tongue, let there be only two or at most three, and each in turn; and let one interpret. But if there is no one to interpret, let each of them keep silence in church and speak to himself and to God. Let two or three prophets speak, and let the others weigh what is said. If a revelation is made to another sitting by, let the first be silent. For you can all prophesy one by one so that all may learn and all be encouraged; and the spirits of prophets are subject to prophets. For God is not a God of confusion but of peace."

Further on, the whole chapter ends with yet another reminder that confusion is not of God: "So, my brethren, earnestly desire to prophesy, and do not forbid speaking in tongues; but all things should be done decently and in order."

Throughout this whole passage Paul is concerned that the church body be uplifted and that God be glorified—peacefully and without confusion. God never asks ten people to speak forth in tongues in the course of one service—even with interpretations. He doesn't prompt twenty people to prophesy; He is more efficient and concise than that. He sees prophecy as more important than public speaking in tongues, but He emphatically tells the church that they are not to forbid tongues.

Verses 18-19 give wonderful insight into this whole teaching. Here Paul speaks of his own personal experience and says, "I thank God that I speak in tongues more than you all; nevertheless, in church I would rather speak five words with my mind, in order to instruct others, than ten thousand words in a tongue." Paul set forth his priorities for public worship, and these priorities must be weighed with his accompanying command—that the Corinthians not forbid the speaking in tongues.

Sometimes, as I read through the Acts of the Apostles and notice the power and authority with which Paul spoke, I'm convinced that he must have privately prayed ten thousand words in the Spirit for every five he publicly spoke with his mind. And that is what I wish for every one of God's children.

Afterword

In Spirit
and In Truth

Our study of the Holy Spirit began with the conversation Jesus had with a Samaritan woman. But there, in the first chapter, I discussed only part of the story presented in John 4.

When Jesus tried to change the topic from physical or even spiritual thirst to personal morality, the woman immediately veered the conversation off onto less threatening ground. When Jesus rightly informed her that He knew she'd had five husbands and that she was living with a sixth man to whom she wasn't married, He'd stepped too close for her comfort. She answered, "I perceive that you are a prophet. Our fathers worshiped on this mountain; and you say that Jerusalem is the place where men ought to worship." Instead of talking about her personal life, she pointed out one of the theological differences between the Jews and the Samaritans.

Jesus, a wise and sensitive man, didn't press the matter of her sin, but accepted her play and discussed the matter of worship. He said, "Woman, believe me, the hour is coming when neither on this mountain nor in Jerusalem will you worship the Father....The hour is coming, and now is, when the true worshipers will worship the Father in spirit and truth, for such the Father seeks to worship him. God is spirit, and those who worship him must worship in spirit and truth."[1]

According to the Jewish law, all the males who lived within a wide radius of Jerusalem had to go to the city three times a year to worship. Centuries before, when the children of Israel had gone into the Promised Land, the Lord had established one place for worship. People were not allowed to offer sacrifices in Bethlehem or Nazareth or Emmaus. The Samaritans, on the other hand, said that Mount Gerizim, near where this conversation took place, was the true place of worship. But here Jesus was saying that the time had come for believers to worship and praise anywhere, anytime—with their spirits.

Now worship is broader than praise, but praise is surely an important part of worship. I thought everyone had a clear understanding of what praise was all about until one day when a student of mine, somewhat agitated, came up to me and said, "I could never believe in a God who sits somewhere on a remote throne demanding the praise of His people. What kind of God is that?"

He got me thinking about the purpose of praise. This young man was asking a good question. Like him, I didn't particularly want to have anything to do with a god who was like the wicked queen in "Snow White," standing before a mirror asking whether or not she was the fairest in the land. I'd met too many irksome people who needed constant assurance of their physical beauty or their inspired ideas or their useful help. If God was like them, He was not big enough or secure enough to be my God.

Then I thought of the groupies who tend to swarm around famous or wealthy people and lavish praise on them to gain their favor or maybe their money. Could the church be a group that hovers around God, telling Him how wonderful He is so they can extract His blessings? When I thought of that, I groaned. If I ever saw that happening in a church, I'd walk out. Real praise has nothing at all to do with flattery.

Then what is real praise? Genuine praise, I believe, is the overflow of enjoyment that wells up from and out of our spirits. It's like the experience of a man in my church who likes to jog. I haven't the slightest idea why someone would want to get up before daylight and run down one street and up another, all around town; but that's what he does. As you might expect, he commends this activity to everybody he meets—and with evangelical zeal. His praise of jogging comes naturally to him, and, actually, it's what we all expect of him because we all know that everyone tends to praise what he or she enjoys. Nobody has to tell a young man to praise the virtues of his girlfriend or a sailor to praise his new boat.

Now, if we have no delight in our Lord, we have no real praise, and if we have no real praise, our worship is empty. The Episcopal hymnbook includes a hymn that says:

In vain we tune our formal songs,

In vain we strive to rise,
Hosannas languish on our tongues,
And our devotions die.[2]

Unfortunately, those words aptly describe what goes on in many churches. The Episcopal Church describes the communion service as a "celebration of Holy Communion" and the presiding priest is called the celebrant, but if you went into some of those churches you'd never guess that you were participating in a celebration. A memorial, perhaps, but not a celebration. And it has nothing to do with worshipping God in spirit and in truth.

Actually, there was nothing new about Jesus' comment to the Samaritan woman. In Isaiah 1, the Lord had said, in effect, "I hate your worship. I can't stand your singing, and your prayers make me sick. What in the world do you think you're doing here, trampling my courts?"

Why was God upset? Because the people of Israel honored Him with their lips but not with their hearts. They had the truth, but they kept it on ice.

I've never forgotten a story I heard about a father and his little son who were sitting on the front pew of the church. The child was restless to say the least. One minute he was on the floor, underneath the seat and looking up at the people sitting in the second row; the next minute he was standing on the pew looking down on them. The father kept saying, "Sit still." But the kid didn't pay any attention until the father grabbed him by the shoulders and sat him down hard. The little boy knew his time had come, but he looked up and said, "I'm sitting down on the outside, but I'm still standing up on the inside."

Afterword

What a perfect illustration of the disparity between outward appearances and inward realities. God is not nearly as concerned with our external postures as He is with our internal attitudes.

Matthew 15 also gives more insight into the kind of worship that has nothing to do with God's truth. Here the Pharisees complained to Jesus because His disciples were breaking the traditions of washing their hands before they ate. Now this wasn't an issue of cleanliness but of ritual and ceremony that was mandated by Jewish elders—not by the Word of God. So Jesus didn't answer their question, but instead asked another one: "Why do *you* break the law of God?"

To make sure they understood, He gave them a specific example: The temple priests had come up with a way around the commandment to honor one's father and mother. They'd said that if you gave to the temple the money you would have used to support your parents, you'd be free of that family obligation.

Jesus quoted Isaiah in judgment of their behavior: "In vain do they worship me, teaching as doctrines the precepts of men."[3] He was telling them that their worship was in vain if they saw their human-made order of worship, church or social structure as God's law.

Believe me, that still happens today. Some years ago a small Episcopal church said good-bye to their long-time rector who was retiring and welcomed a new young man as their priest. But immediately, even after the very first services, the new rector— no matter how hard he tried to please the people—realized that he was somehow offending them. He could see the disapproval in their faces and in their mannerisms.

In time, the senior warden came to talk to the young

priest and admitted that there was a problem. He said, "Father, your predecessor always observed a part of the liturgy that you aren't observing, and the congregation is bothered about this omission."

The pastor was curious, because he wasn't aware that anything was amiss. "What did he do that I'm not?" he asked.

"Well," the warden continued, "right before he started to serve the wine from the chalice, he walked over to the side of the sanctuary and touched the radiator. The people are upset that you're leaving this out."

The priest had never heard of such a tradition, so he called the former pastor and said, "You know I haven't been here very long, but it seems I'm already in trouble and it has something to do with touching the radiator before serving the chalice. I don't remember learning anything about this in seminary. Could I have missed something?"

The older man had a perfectly reasonable explanation. "Oh, no," he said. "I've just done that for years to discharge the static electricity before I put the chalice up to their lips. I didn't want anyone to get a shock."

I've ever since called that church the Church of the Holy Radiator! On one level this extreme but true story is funny, but on another, it's heart-breaking. It illustrates the kind of worship that God calls vain and empty.

True Worship

God accepts only one kind of worship, and it's described again in Romans 12:1: "I appeal to you therefore, brethren, by the mercies of God, to present your bodies as a living sacrifice, holy and acceptable to God, which is your spiritual worship." Ultimately, the only thing God wants from us is ourselves. Of course, that includes everything; but that's what He wants.

So what does it mean to "worship in spirit and truth," as Jesus said? What is our "spiritual worship," as Paul said? A small part of the story of our church, St. Paul's parish, may give you an idea of what such worship is all about.

For months before I arrived as the rector, committees had been planning the yearly stewardship canvass, asking members for their financial pledge. You probably have to be Episcopalian to know what a big deal this is; it's woven into the church's fabric. The canvass was to take place on my third Sunday there, and the Holy Spirit gave me no peace about this pledge drive.

Being so new to the scene and being a good Episcopalian, I told the Lord that if we could just let it pass this time around, I would do what I could to move in another direction the following year. But the Holy Spirit made it perfectly clear to me that my alternative was not acceptable. He was the head of the church; I was simply there to do His will. And if I didn't want to do it, I might as well get out.

Well, I talked to the proper committee, and on the designated Sunday I stood up and said, "You know, I've learned that it is utterly impossible to tip God. We can't casually approach Him and give Him whatever change is in our pockets. And neither can we bribe him or buy him off with our big checks."

Then I got even braver and said, "I'm not asking you how much you're going to pledge to St. Paul's this year, but whether or not you've consciously presented yourself as a living sacrifice. If you don't want to do that, then I beg you not to give one penny to this church. If you can't give Him your life, don't fool yourself into thinking that He will receive anything else you might give Him."

I heard gasps in the congregation. That wasn't the kind of talk they were used to hearing, but that was the very day on which numerous people in that parish started to take their faith seriously. People became aware that God demands commitment, and many were able to say, "Here I am, Lord—broken, battered and in need. Do whatever You can with me."

I sometimes tell my parishioners that the most solemn moment in a worship service is when they walk out through the doorways. Right then they make a decision about whether they're going to leave the Lord behind in the church, or appropriate His presence and power in their lives during the week, becoming worshippers in spirit and in truth with their lives on the altar.

In spirit and in truth. What a wonderful phrase to describe how we're to respond to the Spirit who is truth, the Spirit who resides within us and claims us as His own, who quenches our thirst—who deserves nothing but our best.

I could think of no better way to end a book about the work of the Holy Spirit than by pointing out Ephesians 1:13-14, which gives one of the most encouraging descriptions of Him found anywhere in the New Testament. The Spirit, Paul said, is "the guarantee of our inheritance until we acquire possession of it, to the praise of his glory."

In short, the Holy Spirit is God's down payment on our inheritance. Can you imagine? If the down payment is the Holy Spirit, what can the inheritance be like? We,

the children of God, will someday be heirs to everything
our sovereign Father possesses.
And I mean everything.

Scripture
References

Chapter One

1. John 4:1-18
2. Psalm 42:1-2
3. Psalm 63:1-2
4. John 7:37 (KJV)
5. John 6:51
6. John 7:39
7. John 16:14
8. John 15:26

Chapter Two

1. Mark 1:15
2. Matthew 6:33
3. John 18:36
4. Matthew 7:21
5. Luke 17:33
6. John 3:5
7. Luke 1:31

8. Ephesians 2:8-9
9. 1 Corinthians 12:3

Chapter Three

1. John 3:10
2. Genesis 2:16-17
3. Isaiah 59:2
4. Hebrews 8:7
5. Genesis 22:1-14
6. Hebrews 11:17-19
7. Exodus 13:21
8. Deuteronomy 5:28-29
9. Nehemiah 9:30
10. Hebrews 9:22
11. 1 Samuel 10:6

Chapter Four

1. Acts 10:38
2. Matthew 13:54-56
3. Acts 10:38
4. John 1:29
5. John 19:30
6. Mark 14:24
7. Ezekiel 36:26-28
8. Galatians 4:6-7
9. Genesis 2:7
10. Ezekiel 37
11. 1 Corinthians 3:16-17
12. 1 Corinthians 6:19-20

Chapter Five

1. John 16:7
2. Isaiah 9:6
3. Philippians 2:6-7
4. John 11:21
5. Deuteronomy 6:4; Mark 12:29

6. John 14:26; 15:26
7. John 14:26
8. John 16:13
9. Genesis 1:2
10. 1 Timothy 3:6
11. 1 Kings 19:11-12
12. 1 John 4:4

Chapter Six

1. James 1:13
2. 1 Corinthians 10:13
3. Job 1
4. 1 John 1:8
5. Romans 7:22
6. Romans 7:24-25; 8:1
7. 1 John 1:9; 2:1
8. Isaiah 38:17
9. Psalm 103:12
10. Jeremiah 31:34
11. Romans 8:5
12. Galatians 5:16-18
13. Galatians 5:19-21
14. Galatians 5:22

Chapter Seven

1. Luke 24:49
2. Acts 1:5
3. Acts 1:8
4. Acts 2:22-38
5. Ephesians 6:17
6. Acts 9:1-18

Chapter Eight

1. Isaiah 64:6
2. James 2:14-17
3. Jeremiah 1:4-6

4. Jeremiah 29:11
5. Matthew 25:14-30

Chapter Nine

1. Mark 6:5-6
2. 1 Kings 18,19
3. John 21:22

Chapter Ten

1. Exodus 4:16
2. 1 Corinthians 14:29
3. 1 Corinthians 14:3
4. Jeremiah 23:21-22
5. Jeremiah 23:28-29
6. Luke 7:33
7. 1 Corinthians 14:2
8. 1 Corinthians 14:14
9. 1 Corinthians 14:5
10. 1 Corinthians 12:29
11. 1 Corinthians 12:28

Afterword

1. John 4:20-24
2. "Come, Holy Spirit, Heavenly Dove" by Isaac Watts (1707).
3. Matthew 15:1-9

QUOTED FROM RSV

John 4:10-13, 17-18
Psalm 42:1-2
Psalm 63:1-2
John 7:37
John 6:51
John 7:39
John 16:14
John 15:26

Scripture References

John 3:2-6, 8, 10
Ephesians 5:25-26
1 Peter 1:23
Mark 1:15
Matthew 7:21
Luke 1:31
Ephesians 2:8-9
Romans 10:13,17
Genesis 2:16-17
Exodus 13:21
Deuteronomy 5:28-39
Nehemiah 9:30
Hebrews 9:22
1 Samuel 10:6
Genesis 1:2
Hebrews 1:1
Jeremiah 31:31-33
Genesis 12:1-3
Genesis 17:1-7
Genesis 22:2
Exodus 34:27
Judges 3:10
Judges 11:29
Judges 14:19
Isaiah 11:1
Isaiah 42:1-2
Joel 2:28
Acts 10:38
Matthew 13:54-56
Acts 10:38
John 1:29
John 19:30
Mark 14:24
Ezekiel 36:26-28
Galatians 4:6-7
Genesis 2:7
1 Corinthians 3:16-17
1 Corinthians 6:19-20
Galatians 4:4-7

Isaiah 53:5,10
1 John 3:8
2 Corinthians 5:21
John 5:22
Matthew 27:50-51
1 Timothy 2:5
Romans 10:3
John 20:19-22
John 16:7
Isaiah 9:6
Philippians 2:6-7
Deuteronomy 6:4
John 14:26
John 16:13
1 Kings 19:11-12
1 John 4:4
1 Corinthians 2:11
1 Corinthians 2:12,16
John 14:6,9
John 1:18
John 15:14-15
1 Corinthians 12:3
2 Timothy 1:13
James 1:13
1 John 1:8
Romans 7:22
Romans 7:24,25; 8:1
1 John 1:9; 2:1
Romans 8:5
Galatians 5:16-23
James 1:2
Matthew 4:1
1 John 3:9-10
John 16:9
Exodus 31:1
1 Corinthians 12:1,4,5,7-11,
  28-30,13
Ephesians 2:10
Acts 13:2,4,5

Scripture References

Exodus 3:10; 4:10
1 Corinthians 14:1-6,14,26-33,
   40,18-19
Matthew 25:23,27
Acts 8:19,20
Exodus 7:1-2
2 Peter 1:20-21
1 John 4:1-3
1 Corinthians 14:32
Jeremiah 23:16-18
Romans 8:26-28
Ephesians 6:18
Luke 24:49
Acts 1:5
Acts 1:8
Acts 2:22-38
Jeremiah 1:4-6
Mark 6:5-6
Exodus 4.16
Jeremiah 23:21-22; 28-29
Luke 7:35
John 4:20-24
Romans 12:1
Matthew 15:9
Ephesians 1:14
Isaiah 40:6 7

OTHER PUBLICATIONS OF INTEREST FROM CREATION HOUSE

The Emerging Christian Woman
by Anne Gimenez

Women are on the move. They are shaking off many years of unbiblical silence and passivity. Inspired by the Spirit, they are assuming their proper roles of leadership in the body of Christ. Anne believes Christ is calling Christian women to take a lead in bringing new life, healing and unity to the church. $4.95

Spiritual Power and Church Growth
by C. Peter Wagner

Why do some churches grow like wildfire? How can we learn from this marvelously successful church growth movement? C. Peter Wagner identifies the main reasons for the expansion of Pentecostal churches and articulates key principles behind their growth in Latin America. With examples, stories and facts, he writes about how to engage the power of the Holy Spirit; involving new Christians in ministry; cell groups; training leaders in service; the importance of signs and wonders; and other valuable principles. $6.95

Youth Pastor's Handbook

A unique reference tool for busy youth leaders. This three-ring binder is full of practical and helpful information to make your youth meetings and projects successful.
$25.00

Available at your Christian bookstore or from:

Creation House
190 N. Westmonte Drive
Altamonte Springs, FL 32714